Walks IN West Cheshire AND Wirral

Beeston Castle

Walks IN West Cheshire AND Wirral

Thirty circular walks through the green and varied countryside of West Cheshire and Wirral

Jen Darling
*with significant help from
Martin Banfield*

Mara Books
www.northerneyebooks.co.uk

First published in 1988 by Sigma Leisure, Wilmslow
Revised and updated in 2007, 2010 & 2020 by
Northern Eye Books
Tattenhall, Cheshire, CH3 9PX

This fully revised Third Edition published in 2023 by:
Mara Books
22, Crosland Terrace, Helsby, Cheshire WA6 9LY

www.northerneyebooks.co.uk

ISBN 978 1 902512 36 5

For sales enquiries, please telephone: 01928 723 744

Copyright © Jen Darling 2023

Jen Darling has asserted her right under the Copyright, Designs and Patents Act, 1988 to be identified as the author of this work.
All rights reserved.

Maps: Neil Rogers

Layout and cover design: Carl Rogers

A CIP catalogue record for this book is available from the British Library.

Whilst every effort has been made to ensure that the information in this book is correct at the time of publication, neither the author nor the publisher can accept any responsibility for any errors, loss or injury, however caused.

The routes described in this book are undertaken at the individual's own risk. The publisher and copyright owners accept no responsibility for any consequences arising from the use of this book, including misinterpretation of the maps and directions.

Maps based on out of copyright Ordnance Survey mapping, aerial photographs and local knowledge.

Printed and bound in the UK.

When I first became editor of Cheshire Life, many years ago, Jen Darling was the lady who strolled through our lovely county with her monthly walk, which was one of the regular and much-loved features of Cheshire Life magazine.

As a rookie editor and veteran Cheshire rambler myself, I admired her eye for detail, sense of history and ability to share the thrills and spills of a particular walk, not just with those who followed in her footsteps, but also with the thousands who didn't, but enjoyed the walk in their imagination from the comfort of their own armchair.

For these reasons I feel privileged to endorse *Walks in West Cheshire and Wirral*, an intriguing and challenging journey on foot through the highways and byways of our beloved county.

And, as always when you stride with Jen, you stroll with the darling of Cheshire walkers.

— PATRICK O'NEILL, ONE-TIME EDITOR OF 'CHESHIRE LIFE'

Acknowledgments

My heartfelt thanks to Les Goulding for the long-term loan of all his up-to-date Cheshire and Wirral maps, to Barbara Holloway of The Poplars, Crowton, for providing us with a short-term base for our caravan, to Mary Allen and the Rickety Ramblers for feedback on various walks, and to Chris Darling for his unstinting support and computer expertise.

Photographs

Tony Bowerman, Carl Rogers, John Cocks for 'Cheshire Life', Chris Darling, Jon Morris, David Potts, John Street, Joe Wainwright, Brentwood Arts in Stockton Heath, Clint Hughes/Cheshire County Council, English Heritage.

Contents

From the Author 8
About Cheshire 9

North Cheshire
1. Appleton 6 miles/9.5 km 18
2. Daresbury 4 miles/6.5 km 25
3. Dunham Massey 4 miles/6.5 km 30
4. Grappenhall 4 miles/6.5 km 34
5. Lymm 5 miles/8 km 39
6. Preston-on-the Hill 3 miles/5 km 44
7. Thelwall 4 miles/6.5 km 47

South Cheshire
8. Brown Knowl 3 miles/5 km 51
9. Bunbury 7 miles/11 km 55
10. Grindley Brook 5 miles/8 km 61
11. Malpas 5 miles/8 km 65
12. Peckforton 4 miles/6.5 km 69
13. Rawhead 4 miles/6.5 km 74
14. Tarporley 6 miles/9.5 km 78

Mid Cheshire
15. Davenham 4 miles/6.5 km 84
16. Great Budworth 6.5 miles/10.5 km 88
17. Little Budworth 5.5 miles/9 km 95
18. Little Leigh 5 miles/8 km 100
19. Lower Whitley 3 miles/5 km 104
20. Plumley 4 miles/6.5 km 107

About Cheshire

West Cheshire

21.	Acton Bridge 5 miles/8 km	112
22.	Alvanley 3 miles/5 km	117
23.	Delamere Forest 6 miles/9.5 km	122
24.	Frodsham 4 miles/6.5 km	127
25.	Kingsley 6 miles/9.5 km	132
26.	Primrosehill Wood 5.5 miles/9 km	137

Chester and Wirral

27.	Burton 5 miles/8 km	141
28.	Christleton 4 miles/6.5 km	146
29.	Thornton Hough 3 miles/5 km	151
30.	Thurstaston 7 miles/11 km	155
About the Author		160

From the Author

West Cheshire Walks — as it was then called—was first published in 1988 when, amazingly, there were no other Cheshire walking books on the market. It has sold well ever since, and I am grateful to *Northern Eye Books* for agreeing so readily to publish a new edition in 2007, which included many new walks in the south of Cheshire and Wirral. And now, in 2022, Mara Books has published this totally updated 3rd edition.

It is always fascinating to redo all the walks from the original book. Such a lot has altered in Cheshire during the last 34 years, and it has brought home to me what a changing landscape we inhabit. All the routes have been modified in some way, some enormously. Walks that now pass through huge housing estates or near noisy motorways, have been removed. Many have only needed slight alterations this time.

I am grateful to all those who have bought the book before and hope that many will also enjoy this new, revised edition. The walks vary between 3-7 miles/5-11 kilometres. Certain walkers have also commented that age has caught up with them and long walks are now out of the question. I have made a note of this and short-cuts can now be taken on many of the longer routes.

Maps. Undoubtedly the best maps for walkers are the orange-covered Ordnance Survey 1:25,000 Explorer series. At a scale of 2½ inches to the mile, or 4cm to the kilometre, they show field boundaries and other useful details omitted from the 1:50,000 Landranger maps. Many of the Explorer maps are double-sided and all show the entire public rights of way network, as well as permissive paths and Open Access Land. Almost all of Cheshire is covered by seven maps; with just four core maps covering the walks in this book: 257, *Crewe & Nantwich*; 266, *Wirral & Chester*; 267, *Northwich & Delamere Forest*; and 276, *Bolton, Wigan & Warrington*.

About Cheshire

History. There is evidence of settlement in Cheshire from early times, as shown by Iron Age forts on Woodhouse Hill, above Frodsham, and Maiden Castle, further south. Chester, or *Deva*, was an important Roman settlement and legionary fortress; Northwich, or *Condate*, dates from the same period. A superb example of a medieval castle can still be explored at Beeston.

Industry. One large industrial area is along the River Mersey where the Stanlow Oil Refinery was established by Shell near Ellesmere Port in 1924. The massive cooling towers of Fiddlers Ferry power station on the outskirts of Widnes also dominate the northern skyline.

Salt has been produced in Cheshire for over 2,000 years and is said to have 14,000 modern uses. The industry was originally

Two picturesque Cheshire castles: Victorian Peckforton in the foreground, with medieval Beeston beyond

centred around the three 'wiches'—Northwich, Nantwich and Middlewich—and near Winsford, where rock salt is still mined today for use on our roads in winter.

Waterways. Rivers and canals feature in many of the walks.

The River Mersey once formed the natural boundary between Lancashire and Cheshire and is navigable for 19 miles from its estuary at Liverpool upstream to Warrington. The suspension bridge joining Widnes to Runcorn is a splendid sight. Opened in 1961, it replaced the earlier transporter bridge and was, at the time, the longest in Europe. An old Cheshire rhyme says:

The Weaver, the Peover, the Wheelock and Dane,
When they all meet together they change their name.

They are all tributaries of the Mersey.

The River Weaver lies completely in Cheshire. Rising close to the village of Peckforton, it enters the River Mersey near Frodsham. Made navigable in the 18th century to carry salt downstream for export from Liverpool, it aimed to profit by charging tolls to users.

Now known as the Weaver Navigation, by 1732 barges of 35 tons could travel from the River Mersey to Winsford and by 1880 huge amounts of white and rock salt were annually shipped downstream to Liverpool, then on to other parts of the world. Chemicals were also transported from the huge ICI works complex at Northwich. In 1984, the largest ship ever to navigate the River Weaver came from Holland and weighed 1,080 tons.

Today, the Weaver Navigation can still carry sea-going vessels of over 600 tons and the river is navigable for 20 miles from Winsford to the Manchester Ship Canal at Runcorn. Yet, although it is one of the country's last commercial waterways, its use has declined as road transport has taken much of its trade. All the locks along its course, however, are still manned by keepers.

The Dee estuary is a priceless and beautiful wilderness and a place of international importance, it being a vital staging post during the spring and autumn migration of many birds. The vast area of mud flats and salt marsh also form an important breeding ground for shelduck, oystercatcher, black-headed gull and redshank. And the many waders and ducks, which overwinter here, include large flocks of pintail, teal, mallard, wigeon and shelduck. The marshland is also home to the natterjack toad.

The Manchester Ship Canal is visible from high ground on several walks. Queen Victoria opened it in 1894 when she sailed up its length from Liverpool to Manchester. Almost 37 miles long, it has five locks and several large swing bridges, such as the three at Warrington. (The rival to these is over the River Weaver a little further south on the A49 at Acton Bridge.) The Ship Canal was directly responsible for making Manchester into one of Britain's largest seaports, despite being 32 miles from the coast, and an enormous amount of industry grew up along its banks.

The Runcorn-Widnes suspension bridge's graceful arc soars above the River Mersey

The Bridgewater Canal was completed in 1776. James Brindley was engaged to design and construct this canal and lived to see it finished as far as Stockton Heath. At the time there were no railways and transport by road was expensive because of tolls and poor surfaces. It was the first canal to be built that didn't follow an existing water course, and is all on one level with no locks but some aqueducts.

Horse-drawn boats first carried the Duke of Bridgewater's coal in bulk, and safely, some 28 miles from his mines at Worsley, through Manchester to the Mersey estuary opposite Liverpool, which it entered via a series of locks. A passenger service was also developed, which was well used up to the 1920s. Today, the canal has a new lease of life for pleasure boats and fishermen.

The Shropshire Union Canal was first opened in 1795. It was constructed at a time of rapid canal building known as 'canal mania', when waterways were built to link the estuaries of the Rivers Mersey, Thames, Severn and Humber to transport bulky low value goods, such as coal, iron and limestone across the country. Thomas Telford was the engineer responsible for much of the work and the main route extends from Ellesmere Port to Chester, then across the Cheshire Plain and on through Staffordshire to Wolverhampton.

The scenic Llangollen Canal branches off at Hurleston Junction, where four locks raise it 34 feet. It then wends its way through the rolling Cheshire countryside to Wrenbury and Grindley Brook, before winding through Shropshire and entering Wales at Chirk. It then continues across the dizzying height of the Pontcysyllte Aqueduct before its final stretch into Llangollen.

The Trent & Mersey Canal, originally known as the Grand Trunk Canal, was constructed in 1776 to facilitate transport from the Staffordshire Potteries to the River Mersey and Manchester. 93 miles long, it starts at Shardlow on the River Trent and joins the Bridgewater Canal at Preston Brook. James Brindley designed this waterway but died before it was completed. The Duke of Bridgewater backed it, as did the famous potter, Josiah Wedgwood, and one of its functions was to transport china clay, which was first shipped up from Cornwall to Liverpool. The canal was built to take wide beam boats, many of them built in Northwich.

The Countryside. Cheshire is sometimes described as a region of parks and meres. Much of its parkland belonged originally to estates owned by families for generations, some having now been gifted to The National Trust. The estate villages and tenant farms are always well-maintained and often have distinctive characteristics.

There are many meres, both natural and man-made. Known as 'flashes', those around Northwich have been caused by salt subsidence. Mosses are another common habitat where peaty ground has formed woodland or marsh.

An original cast-iron mile post on the Trent & Mersey Canal

Cheshire is noted for its sunken lanes with high banks on either side, often topped by hedgerows. Hawthorn predominates, although other plants, such as blackthorn, wild rose and elder, can often be seen. Well-established hedges surrounding fields will often have mature trees, particularly oaks, growing from them at intervals, to provide shelter for cattle.

Ponds for watering cattle can still be seen in many Cheshire fields. Many of these are disused marl pits. Deposits of a black clay called marl were dug out and spread over the rest of the field to enrich the sandy soil. Gangs of men known as 'marlers' used to go from farm to farm to excavate and spread it. The hollow left behind then filled with rainwater and became known as a marl pit.

The rich soil on the plain provides excellent pastureland for dairy farming and herds of Friesian cattle can still be seen. Cheshire cheese used to be made on the farms, but is now mostly made in factories. Farm buildings, often grouped in rectangles, survive from the 18th and 19th centuries.

Georgian houses, as at Christleton, were made of bricks from local clay found on the Cheshire Plain. Red sandstone was also quarried to provide building material for houses, bridges and churches, many of which still survive.

Many Cheshire cottages are faced with white plaster inset in black beams of oak. Often referred to as 'magpie' buildings, some are very old. Examples can be found in the picturesque villages of Peckforton and Beeston, but you will notice them dotted all over the countryside, some still having thatched roofs.

Churches too abound and many villages are dominated by their Anglican church. Examples are the great Perpendicular

A seventeenth-century half-timbered black-and-white cottage in Beeston village, below Beeston Castle

churches at Great Budworth and Bunbury, and the soaring spire at Oughtrington. Daresbury too has its special connection with the famous author, Lewis Carroll.

The Woodland Trust, working with local people, created 200 new community woods across England and Wales, to mark the Millennium in 2000. Three of the walks encompass these – Grappenhall Wood, Spud Wood at Lymm, and the Lewis Carroll memorial woodland near Preston-on-the Hill.

Wirral Country Park opened in 1973 and was Britain's first country park. It is a linear park, converted from the once busy railway line which linked Hooton, on the main Chester to Birkenhead line, to West Kirby. 12 miles long, the line closed in 1962 and the track then lay derelict for several years.

It was the vision of a local resident, Laurence Beswick, that saw the creation of this linear way, which provides recreation, conservation and education for so many. The stations have been converted into car parks and picnic spots, and the visitor centre is based at Thurstaston station.

The Sandstone Trail follows the ridge which intermittently bisects the Cheshire plain from north to south. Starting from Frodsham and ending at Whitchurch, it runs for over 30 miles and several walks incorporate part of it. The trail enjoys a variety of scenery, from the Overton Hills above Frodsham, through Delamere Forest to the craggy slopes around Rawhead (its highest point) after which it finishes through lush pastureland.

The South Cheshire Way stretches for 32 miles across the south of the county, from Grindley Brook in the west to Mow Cop in the east. It also links the Sandstone and Gritstone Trails.

The Timberland Trail covers 22 miles from Runcorn Hill to Spud Wood, near Lymm, following the often wooded sandstone ridge overlooking the Mersey valley, but sometimes descending to the valley floor. Providing views at both levels, it passes over Windmill Hill and Daresbury Firs, drops down to Appleton Reservoir, The Dingle and Grappenhall Wood, then takes in the Bridgewater Canal and Lymm Dam.

The Trans-Pennine Trail is over 120 miles in length. Developed as a recreational route for walkers and cyclists, it stretches from Liverpool to Hull, linking the Irish Sea to the North Sea via Southport, Warrington, Manchester, Barnsley and Leeds.

The Bishop Bennet Way, a 34 mile route for horse riders, uses mainly bridleways and country lanes. It starts near Beeston Castle, then runs west towards the Welsh border, passing Tattenhall and Aldford then turning south to Farndon and Malpas before ending near Whitchurch.

Born in 1745 in the Tower of London, William Bennet became a bishop and member of the House of Lords. But each summer he traversed the ancient tracks, carrying out some of the earliest detailed surveys of Roman roads, including those between Chester (*Deva*) and Whitchurch (*Mediolanum*). He died in 1820.

The Countryside Code
The simplified Countryside Code reflects new open access rights and social changes over the last 20 or so years.
- Be safe. Plan ahead and follow any signs.
- Leave gates and property as you find them.
- Protect plants and animals, and take your litter home.
- Keep dogs under close control.
- Consider other people.

The Walks

1. Appleton

A country walk around the place where the author lived for over 30 years

Appleton Park, Appleton Reservoir, Bridgewater Canal, up the 'rabbit run' to Hill Cliffe, Firs Lane, London Road, then past the Pineways' pond

Start: *Behind the shops in Dudlow Green Road. Map reference: SJ 623845.*

By Car: *Take the A49 south from Warrington and, after passing Warrington Golf Club on your right, turn left into Dudlow Green Road (signposted to Appleton Parish Hall). Park in the large car park on the right, behind the shops.*

Distance: *6 miles/9.5 kilometres.*

Duration: *Allow 3 hours.*

Difficulty: *Mostly easy. One gentle uphill stretch.*

Food and Drink: *Food and drink can be bought at the Co-op, where you park. London Bridge pub (01925 267904) open for food all day, every day. Walton Hall Gardens (01925 601617). The coffee shop sells drinks and snacks.*

Map: *OS 1:25,000 Explorer 276 Bolton, Wigan & Warrington.*

The walk

1. Walk back onto Dudlow Green Road and turn right, passing Limeways before turning right again along a tarmac footpath.

This used to be cobbled and was one of the drives to the now demolished Appleton Hall, home of the Lyon family, once well known local benefactors. Today, relics of their estate, such as iron post-and-rail fencing and cobblestone tracks, can still be found amidst the plethora of modern development.

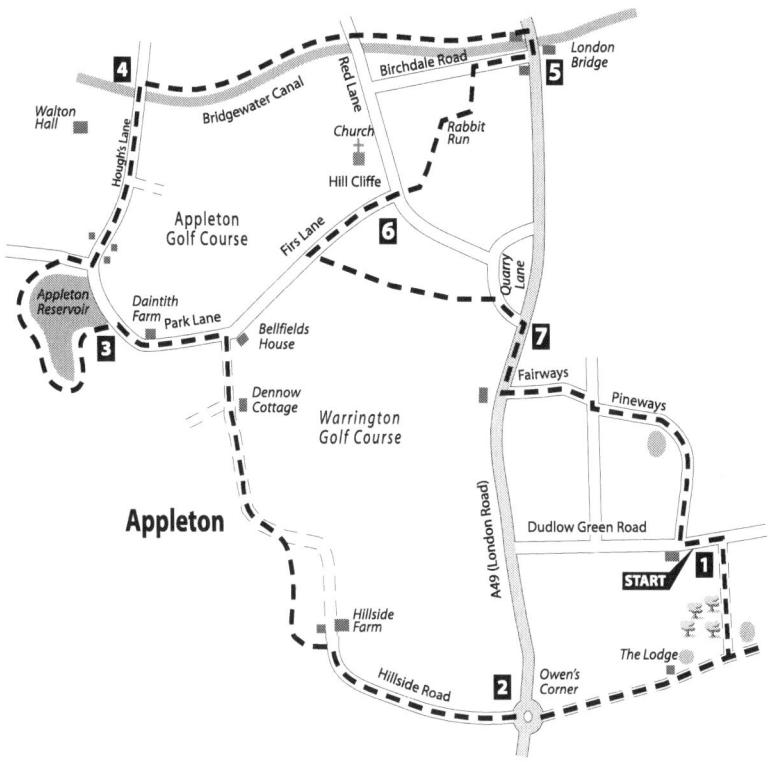

Turn right along a bridleway and you soon pass The Lodge on your right.

Although much extended, this was once a gamekeeper's cottage and is the only lodge on the estate to retain many original features, such as the brickwork, windows, doors and chimney pots.

Continue through an avenue of beech trees, on a path parallel with Pewterspear Lane. In autumn, what a delight to crunch through the fallen leaves.

Stretton Church soon comes into sight. It is said that on a clear day seven counties can be seen from the top of the tower and you may hear its peal of eight bells.

2. Turn right to the roundabout at Owen's Corner and the A49.

Dating from Roman times, the A49 is one of Cheshire's oldest roads, surviving as a medieval route, then a toll road and a busy coach road. Notice the sculpture of the double-faced (male and female) bronze head of the Roman god Janus, positioned on a sandstone column. This god was originally associated with entrances (doors and gates) and it stands where the line of the old Roman road veers away from the A49 towards St Matthew's church, Stretton.

Cross this busy main road with great care and go ahead along Hillside Road. Approaching Hillside Farm, bear left along a footpath (on tarmac at first), which skirts fields all the way to Dennow Cottage. Then keep ahead to Bellfields Farm.

The house called Bellfields was built by Admiral Hoare, a retired naval commander, who modelled it on a ship.

Also notice the sandstone pillar on the grassy triangle. It is supposed to mark the spot where Cromwell's horse was buried, after being killed in a skirmish nearby in 1648.

From here you may also get a glimpse of the spire of Walton Church. In its idyllic setting, the latter is said to have the appearance of a miniature cathedral. The top of the spire is 130 feet/40 metres from the ground and the church was built by Sir Gilbert Greenall late in the 19th century at a cost of £10,000.

Turn left down Park Lane – an extension of Firs Lane – and you soon pass Daintith Farm.

A Mr Daintith was the second minister of Hill Cliffe Baptist Church, so the farm may have been named after him or his family. The farmhouse is very picturesque, built of weathered sandstone slabs, probably quarried locally.

3. For a short detour, turn left up the steps and onto the path round Appleton Reservoir.

This was the original source of water for Warrington and was built in 1846. It still supplies the town with a million gallons/4.5 million litres of water a day for industrial use, and is a delight for both birders and fishermen.

Appleton

Go round the end of the reservoir and back down the opposite bank. Turn right when you reach the road again, then go left down Hough's Lane, signposted to Walton Hall Gardens.

The keeper of the reservoir lived in one of the workmen's cottages, built early in the 20th century, which overlook the filter beds.

Continue down here to Hough's Bridge, which you cross and drop down onto the towpath of the Bridgewater Canal.

The hump-backed bridges here and at Red Lane are original, dating back to when the canal was built in 1776.

4. From here a right turn along the canal leads to Walton Hall Gardens, where refreshments may be available.

However, to continue the walk turn left along the towpath towards Stockton Heath. Banks of flaming gorse festoon the

A bronze bust of Janus, the Roman god of entrances and exits, marks the line of the old Roman road as it heads towards Stretton

slopes on the hillside opposite before you walk under Red Lane Bridge and continue behind houses. Leave the canal before the wide, low arch of London Bridge, turning right and right again up onto it.

Here, Thorn Marine, a ships' chandlery and canal shop which services the many pleasure boats that enjoy this scenic waterway (part of the Cheshire Ring) was under threat of closure in 2006 to make way for yet more housing. The section of the property nearest the bridge used to be two bankriders' cottages. Whatever the weather, these hardy fellows once rode the horses which towed the barges.

From London Bridge you will get the best view of the pub, which dates from the 18th century when the Bridgewater Canal was completed as far as this point. The wharf here was known as Stockton Quay and locals descended the circular flight of steep steps to board the fast passenger boats to Manchester. The fare was 1d a mile and the service only ended in 1918 — the last to be terminated in England.

5. Turn right up London Road (A49) and immediately go right again along Birchdale Road.

The house here, with the small arched window (166 London Road), used to be the customs house and toll keeper's cottage.

Pass Birchdale Crescent then turn left up the footpath – the start of the 'Rabbit Run'.

When our children were small, in the 1970s, we lived on Kingsley Drive and this was a favourite walk. The people who lived in the older houses on the estate then, could remember when the whole area was a grassy hill. However, they said that watching the children was much more fun than seeing the rabbits! Happy days!

Cross the junction of Kingsley Drive and Warren Drive, and walk uphill, on a winding path behind the houses, to Warren Road. Cross this and continue up to Delphfields Road. Dog-leg right and left here, ascending steps to Highwood Road. Turn right, then left at the end up Red Lane, to the imposing black-and-white lychgate of Hill Cliffe Baptist Church.

Cromwell is thought to have worshipped at an early church here and

Built for canal passengers in the eighteenth century, this flight of semi-circular steps can still be seen at Stockton Quay, beside London Bridge

the oldest authentic stone in the ancient burial ground is that of one Maria Heslop, who died in February 1664.

From here there are sweeping views towards Cumbria and along the Mersey valley from Manchester to Liverpool. On a clear day, you can even see Winter Hill and the Pennines. Easy to spot in Warrington is St Elphin's, its parish church, which has one of the tallest church spires in England.

6. From here continue forward into Firs Lane.

The bulky mass on your right holds an underground storage reservoir. Constructed towards the end of the 1960s, it can hold ten million gallons/45 million litres of water.

After passing a semi-bungalow (Whitegates) on the left, turn left down a footpath.

If you first walk forward for a few yards the road winds downhill through eerie sandstone cliffs. Pickmarks are still visible on the lichen-covered walls and the horse trough is a relic from a bygone age.

However, the main walk goes down the footpath, which crosses an estate road, then continues to Quarry Lane, skirting the course of Warrington Golf Club. Turn right along this, which gets its name from the old sandstone quarry behind the houses on your left.

In 1859 the quarry provided stone for the restoration of Warrington parish church, and all the sandstone walls in the area, most of them originally bordering the Lyon estate, were probably built with stone from here.

7. Turn right along the A49, crossing with care then taking the next left turn down Fairways, opposite the golf club entrance. Keep straight on into Pineways and enjoy the wildlife as you skirt the pond.

This is artificial, originally dug out by the Lyon family to enhance their estate. Mallard, coot and moorhen are plentiful, and you may be lucky enough to see a tufted duck or heron. Perch and roach can also sometimes be spotted in the water.

The shops and the end of the walk are now ahead.

When 'West Cheshire Walks' *was first published in 1988 the author lived on Pineways. One day a couple clutching a copy of the book stopped to talk to her husband who was working in the front garden. "And have you heard of the author?" they enquired. "I'm married to her," came the reply, as he trundled off with his wheelbarrow, chortling away at their astonishment.*

2. Daresbury
In the footsteps of Lewis Carroll

Daresbury village, The Firs on Keckwick Hill, Bridgewater Canal, Moore, Outer Wood, All Saints Church

Start: *Small lay-by outside Daresbury church. Map reference: SJ 581828.*

By Car: *Take the A56 from Warrington. Turn left into the village of Daresbury, then go left again down Daresbury Lane. Park opposite the church.*

Distance: *4 miles/6.5 kilometres.*

Duration: *Allow 2 hours.*

Difficulty: *Easy. Perhaps muddy in places.*

Food and Drink: *Red Lion in Moore (01925 740205); Ring o' Bells in Daresbury (01925 740256).*

Map: *OS 1:25,000 Explorer 276 Bolton, Wigan & Warrington.*

The walk

1. Turn towards Hatton, and immediately go right at a footpath sign on the right. Cross the field with the hedge on your left. The kissing gate you are aiming for is in the far right-hand corner. Walk up the right-hand side of the next field until you come to a stile in the hedge by a gate. Turn right over this and go straight ahead, with the hedge on your right, until you reach Old Chester Road. Turn right down it, passing the primary school

*Dating from 1600, it must be one of the oldest still in use in Cheshire and, with all its new extensions since the 1970s when I taught there, it **must** now have inside toilets! The 'Alice in Wonderland' weather vane, which features Alice, the Mad Hatter and White Rabbit, was made by the local blacksmith and was originally erected on the chimney of the smithy. Later, however, it was donated to the school.*

Turn left along the footpath just before Rose Cottage. Can you see the grinning Cheshire Cat on the barn opposite? Keep round the left-hand side of the field going through two kissing gates. Then cross the dual carriageway with great care, climbing up into the field on the other side of this busy road.

Go straight ahead with the hedge on your left until you come to a kissing gate. This leads into Daresbury Firs, an area of Keckwick Hill, where sandstone was quarried for the building of Daresbury church. Instead of walking straight down the hill

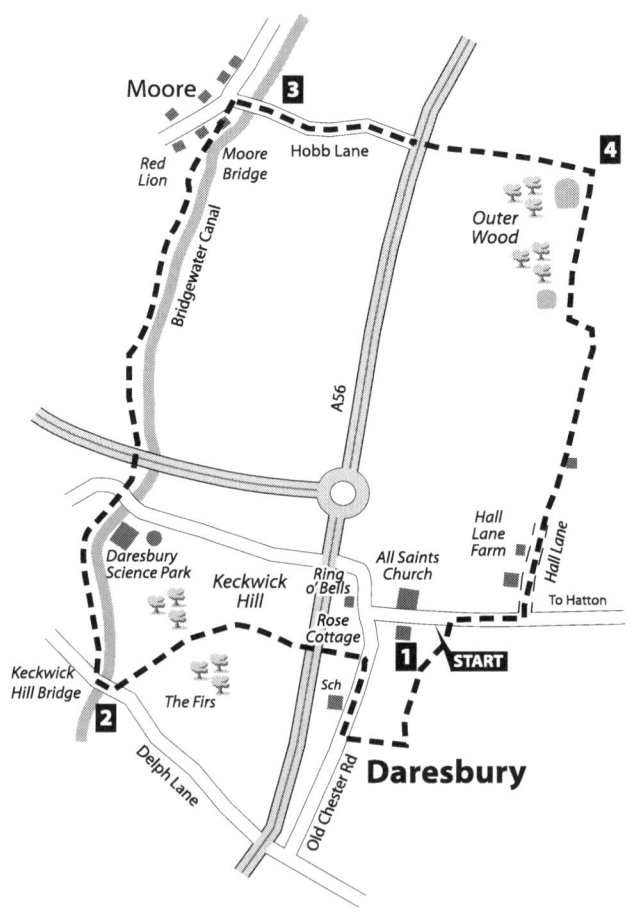

Daresbury

Made by a local blacksmith, this curious weather-vane celebrates Daresbury's connections with Lewis Carroll, author of 'Alice in Wonderland'

from here you may wish to turn left to follow the well-marked path as it zig-zags downhill to the main track. Turn left along this, then continue down the side of a field to reach Delph Lane through a new wooden gate.

Information boards tell you that Daresbury Firs was originally a commercial plantation (a 'tree factory') planted in 1978. Owned by Halton Borough Council since 1996, it is now managed as a community woodland for wildlife, recreation and some timber production.

The evergreens are not actually firs but a mixture of Scots, Corsican and lodgepole pines. The silver birch have simply seeded themselves.

2. Turn right along the lane and cross the Bridgewater Canal over Keckwick Hill Bridge. Drop down to the towpath and turn left along it towards Moore.

You will soon pass what is now the Daresbury International Science and Technology Park. It used to be the Daresbury Nuclear Physics Laboratory – opened by prime minister Harold Wilson in 1967 – and its neat appearance and well-kept grounds are impressive. The distinctive concrete tower was built in 1975 to house a synchrotron radiation source, much to the disgust of local residents at the time.

3. Pass under three bridges before leaving the canal at Moore Bridge. (A left turn here will take you, in 250 metres, to the Red Lion in Moore village.) However, to continue the walk, turn right up Hobb Lane. Cross the busy A56 with extreme caution and walk down the footpath opposite, which soon passes the end of Outer Wood, from where you have a panoramic view of industrial Warrington.

4. Turn right to walk down the wood's side. The very explicit sign, 'Keep out. Trespassers may be accidentally shot!' has disappeared but I would not risk entering. Instead, enjoy the pond life from the perimeter, until you go through a kissing gate and turn left. Follow the hedge round the field to a gate which leads onto Hall Lane, where the blue-and-gold clock on the barn's wooden tower will tell you how long you have been walking.

The squat tower of Daresbury Church soon comes into view. The oldest part of the church, it dates from the 16th century and houses a ground floor ring of eight bells. An unusual rhyme in the ringers' chamber is an acrostic, the initial letters of each line spelling out the word DARESBURY. The church clock has been equipped with Westminster chimes which add further charm to walking in this area.

You will soon reach the rest of Hall Lane Farm and, beyond the farmhouse, keep ahead past a huge holly hedge, to reach Daresbury Lane again, where you turn right to end the walk. However, the hungry and thirsty may like to continue to the Ring o' Bells in the village before returning via All Saints Church.

Opposite the Ring o' Bells is a tiny gate near a bus stop. Cross over the small field and enter the churchyard. Sombrely shaded by yews, the gate here has a modern, automatic shutting device and, like with the sandstone wall, probably dates from 1786.

The church is well worth a visit, and is usually open on weekend afternoons. The Jacobean pulpit is intricately carved and the Lewis Carroll Memorial Window in a side chapel depicts the author with Alice and several of the animals from his famous stories. Can you spot

Fishing on the Bridgewater Canal, with Daresbury Science Park's distinctive concrete tower in the background

the White Rabbit and the Mad Hatter, and the Dormouse is there too, sitting in the teapot, as well as several others?

As you leave the churchyard by the main gate you will also see the font in which Charles Lutwidge Dodgson was baptised.

Daresbury is well known for its associations with Lewis Carroll whose real name was Charles Lutwidge Dodgson. He was the son of a Vicar of Daresbury and spent part of his childhood here. One wonders if this was where his imagination was first kindled into giving odd personalities to rabbits, caterpillars, snails and other creatures.

3. Dunham Massey

A pleasant stroll over fields, through parkland and along a canal

Agden Bridge, River Bollin, Dunham Park, Little Bollington, Bridgewater Canal

Start: Near Agden Bridge. Map reference: SJ 718866.

By Car: *Take the A56 from Lymm towards Altrincham. After the Jolly Thresher traffic lights, take the second left turn down Warringon Lane. Park immediately in the old road on the right. Alternatively, from the motorway exit to Altrincham, take the road to Lymm and Warrington Lane is the next turn on the right after Ye Olde Number Three.*

Distance: *4 miles/6.5 kilometres.*

Duration: *Allow 2 hours.*

Difficulty: *Easy.*

Food and Drink: *The Swan with Two Nicks (0161 928 2914).*

Map: *OS 1:25,000 Explorer 276 Bolton, Wigan & Warrington.*

The walk

1. Walk over Agden Bridge, pass Agden Bridge Farm then turn right over a cattle grid into the road marked 'Woolstencroft Farm'. In front of the farm bear right and continue along a concrete track that may be muddy.

Turn left at the end of the first field through a metal kissing gate (or the main gate) and follow a concrete slatted path. At the field's end turn right through another metal kissing gate, then follow the hedge and exit via a stile in the far corner. (You have now walked round two sides of this field.)

Drop down the rough pasture ahead, cross a small stream and climb up, leaving the field by a sturdy bridge. Rise to a signpost by a power line and continue straight on towards Dunham

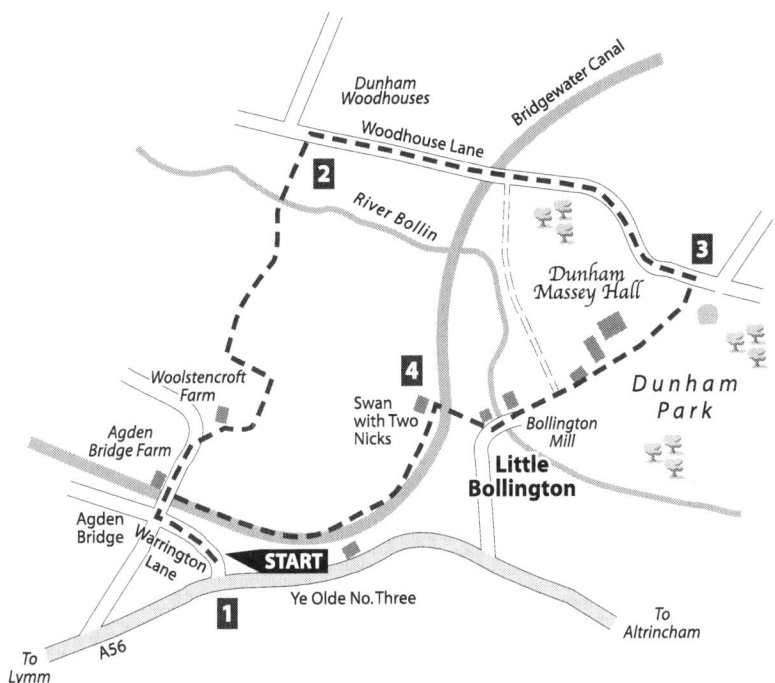

Woodhouses. The right-of-way now follows the power line through a wooden kissing gate at the crest of the slope before veering left down to another bridge. Bear slightly right over the next field to a stile and the River Bollin.

This pleasant little river rises in moorland in the Pennine foothills and flows through Macclesfield, Wilmslow and Bowdon before ending up as one of the chief feeders of the River Mersey and the Manchester Ship Canal about 30 miles/48 kilometres from its source. The attractive Bollin Valley Way follows the river's course.

2. Keep ahead over the river onto a muddy track which becomes Meadow Lane and leads past Bollin Cottages into the village of Dunham Woodhouses.

The cottages in this tiny hamlet were built to house the woodsmen working on the nearby Dunham Massey estate.

When you come to Woodhouse Lane turn right and, after leaving the village, you soon walk under the Bridgewater Canal.

Then continue along the lane, following the high wall past the car park entrance and around the perimeter of the Dunham Massey estate.

The total length of this extensive wall, erected in the mid-18th century, is almost three miles. Look carefully at the brickwork. To give stability, four layers are laid lengthwise, the fifth is end on.

3. Turn right when you reach a cream-painted gate and step-ladder stile and walk ahead through the park, passing the mansion, where you might like to detour to the cafe for a cream cake (highly recommended by my daughter-in-law).

The park is medieval in origin. Over 3,000 new trees have been planted since it was gifted to The National Trust in 1976 and you may be lucky enough to spot the herd of fallow deer.

The hall itself was remodelled in Georgian style in 1732. The stables alongside the house, now housing the shop and cafe, were probably completed in 1721 — the date on the clock turret. The Elizabethan water mill, which had an overshot wheel, dates from 1616, although the Georgian oval windows in the eaves were added in 1756.

Leave the park by another cream step-ladder stile, beyond the water mill renovated early in 2022, and continue ahead, between fields, to the Bollington Mill complex.

Five storeys high, Bollington Mill is an imposing building. Originally a flour mill, it used water diverted from the River Bollin. The river banks above the weir were built up to give a greater head of water and the machinery which operated the sluice gates can still be clearly seen. These controlled the flow of water to the huge undershot wheel, which probably powered four or five millstones on a line shaft. Later, the mill was used as a store for cheese, then fertiliser, before being developed into the luxury apartments you see today.

Cross the mill race by a narrow footbridge and walk into the village of Little Bollington, perhaps pausing for a while at The Swan with Two Nicks.

An attractive watering hole, its name refers to the practice of putting nicks into a swan's beak to establish ownership. At one time the highwayman Dick Turpin is reputed to have been a frequent customer.

An attractive pub, the Swan with Two Nicks takes its name from the ancient practice of marking a swan's beak to establish ownership

Turn right at the small village green, dominated by its oak tree, and follow the cobbled track under the canal before turning right, up steps in the bank.

When the canal was a busy waterway a horse-drawn passenger boat called 'The Packet' stopped at the wharf here at 9am each morning to take people to Manchester, its shrill whistle heralding its arrival.

4. Turn right along the towpath and through the trees you may soon get a glimpse of the small village church, built in gothic style, before passing Ye Olde Number Three.

Reputed to have three ghosts, all friendly, this busy inn got its name from being the third stop for a change of horses for the 'Chester Fliers' – the fast passenger boats which sailed between Chester and Manchester in the 19th century. (The name 'Chester Flier' is now the local nickname for the express diesel trains operating between these two cities.)

After passing under Agden Bridge leave the towpath and return to your car.

4. Grappenhall
A walled garden, woods and a wizard

Hall Lane, Grappenhall Heys, The Firs, Grappenhall village and woodland

Start: *Lay-by near Whitehouse Farm on Broad Lane. Map reference: SJ 641856.*

By Car: *Take the A50 from Warrington towards Knutsford. Approaching the M6, turn right at the first roundabout onto the B5356. At the next roundabout turn right again down Broad Lane. Park on the right in the small lay-by after Whitehouse Farm.*

Distance: *4 miles/6.5 kilometres*

Duration: *Allow 2 hours.*

Difficulty: *Easy. Muddy in places.*

Food and Drink: *Rams Head (01925 262814) and Parr Arms (01925 267393) in Grappenhall village. Cafe in the Walled Garden.*

Map: *OS 1:25,000 Explorer 276 Bolton, Wigan & Warrington.*

The walk

1. Walk forward down the road, cross the stream and turn left down Hall Lane, which soon becomes a grassy track. Pass through a kissing gate and bear left immediately after a small pond. Keep left along this path through deciduous woodland until it eventually turns right alongside a field, and a stream which it crosses several times before a right turn takes you along the path parallel with Lumb Brook Road.

Bear left when you reach an estate road and immediately right on the path behind Dairy Farm, which passes a children's playground. Grappenhall Heys' Walled Garden is immediately ahead, accessed through the archway on your left as you reach Witherwin Avenue.

Check the opening hours of this delightful spot which can now be visited except on a Monday and the cafe is open on Friday, Saturday and Sunday.

The garden was created by wealthy Warrington banker Thomas Parr in about 1830 when he built a house nearby on his family estate. It is unusual because it combines kitchen and pleasure gardens within one walled area. The informal areas are a delight, with paved pathways weaving past ponds, ornamental shrubs and trees, and flower borders.

Fruit, vegetables and flowers grown in the kitchen garden are often for sale. Traditional varieties of pear are trained as espaliers on the west wall and apples are grown in a small orchard. The remains of the extensive glasshouses are backed by buildings used as working and storage space by the gardeners.

After visiting, exit via the entrance gates at the far end. If the walled garden is not open, cross Witherwin Avenue and continue

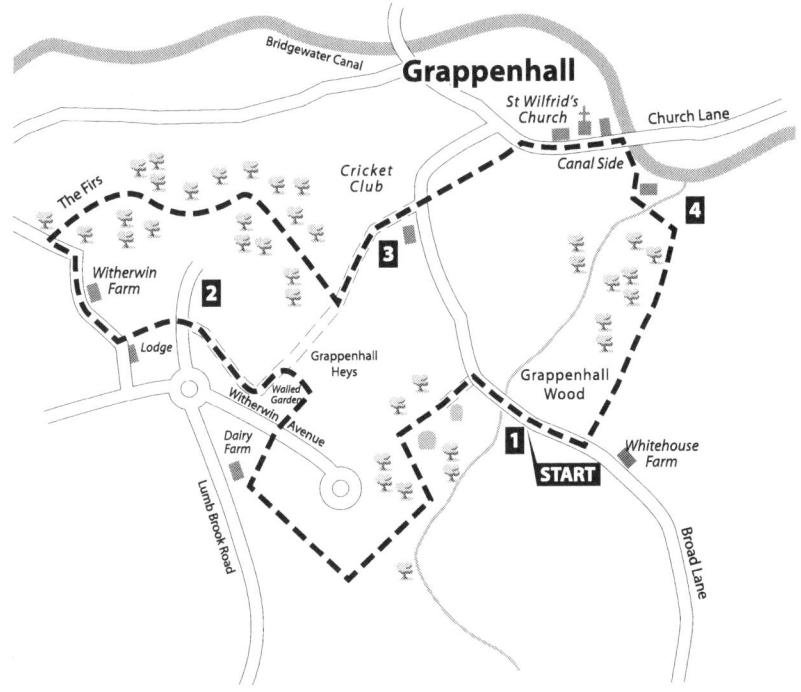

forward, round three sides of the wall. After passing the entrance gates drop down the track through the wood.

You may spot a few remains of the splendid Parr family mansion down here, demolished in 1975, as you walk past ancient yews which still border the track.

2. Exit through ornamental gates onto Astor Drive. Cross this and go ahead down a track to one of the two original lodges on the Parr estate. From here turn right down the road, then right again into Parrs Wood, once known as The Firs.

The fir trees are actually Scots pine and this very mixed woodland is carpeted by bluebells and other wild flowers. Thomas Parr, the original owner of the estate, shut this track to the public on one day every year to prevent it being declared a public right-of-way.

You are now on the Timberland Trail and, on a clear winter's day, may see Winter Hill to the east and Billinge Hill to the north. Prominent local landmarks are the blue-and-white building of Lever Bros. soapworks, the Cheshire Lines warehouse near Central Station, the spire of the parish church, and St Oswald's in Winwick.

Continue along the path, bearing right under huge beech trees until you eventually cross the bridge between a stream and pond. From here bear right up steps and continue, turning left at a steel kissing gate and a signpost to Grappenhall village.

3. Pass Grappenhall Cricket Club, and the second lodge on the Parr estate, to reach Broad Lane once more. Cross it and carry on along the footpath which skirts behind houses. Turn right down Church Lane, which soon becomes cobbled.

You pass the primary school with its many extensions, then the Rams Head which has an unusual sundial set into its sandstone facade. The Parr Arms is the pub next to the church. It is the older of the two and has the Parr family's crest above the door.

The ancient stocks still stand outside the church. Apparently, in the Middle Ages, at a certain time during the Sunday service, the churchwardens left the church and walked along the village street. Anyone found causing a disturbance was put in the stocks for the day.

Grappenhall

Reflections in the Bridgewater Canal enhance Australia Lane, near Grappenhall

 Evidence has been found of a Bronze Age settlement at Grappenhall, and the font in the church may be of Saxon origin. The figure of a cat on the outside wall of the tower – below the ringing chamber window – is said to be the one that gave Lewis Carroll his idea for the Cheshire Cat.

 Continue past the church and, at the Bridgewater Canal, turn right down Canal Side, which leads to Australia Lane. When the house, faintly named Bridgewater, faces you, turn right at the signpost down a narrow path, which crosses a stream and turns right, then through a steel kissing gate into Grappenhall Wood.

 One of 200 planted by the Woodland Trust to celebrate the Millennium, the wood's trees are all native and include oak, ash, silver birch, wild cherry, rowan and hazel, together with dog rose, hawthorn and blackthorn.

Set in a woodland glade, Grappenhall's Wizard of the Woods was carved by local artist, Paul Noon

4. Continue on the path which runs round the perimeter back to another kissing gate and Broad Lane.

For some years this woodland was enhanced by the Wizard of the Woods. 10 feet/3 metres high, this delightful wooden sculpture was devised by local schoolchildren with the help of Paul Noon, a local artist. This benevolent wizard offered shelter to small creatures such as hare, fox, owl, butterfly and ladybird, and leaves and flowers enhanced his clothes. An utter delight, mindlessly set alight by vandals one night.

As you exit back to your car there is a sculpture of a monk holding a ball. Was this supposed to replace the wizard I wonder?

5. Lymm

New woodland and a water tower, The Dam and Dingle, an ancient village cross and the Bridgewater Canal

Spud Wood, Burford Lane, Helsdale Wood, Saint Peter's Church, Higher Lane, Crouchley Lane, Lymm Dam and Dingle, Lymm Cross, Bridgewater Canal

Start: *Spud Wood car park. Map reference: SJ 702874.*

By Car: *Take the A56 from Lymm towards Altrincham and turn left down Oughtrington Lane. After crossing the Bridgewater Canal, turn right onto Stage Lane. The car park is on the right.*

Distance: *5 miles/8 kilometres.*

Duration: *Allow 2 to 3 hours.*

Difficulty: *Easy. Muddy in places.*

Food and Drink: *The Barn Owl (01925 752020), Church Green inn (01925 752068), The Spread Eagle and other pubs in the village.*

Map: *OS 1:25,000 Explorer 276 Bolton, Wigan & Warrington.*

The walk

1. Bear right along the footpath and cross Grantham's Bridge, which used to take a farm track over the canal but now allows entry into Spud Wood – the start of the Timberland Trail.

Spud Wood is a 42-acre/17 hectare site acquired by the Woodland Trust in 1997. 60% is woodland, planted with native trees and shrubs, the rest is wildflower meadows and glades. The original farmland here was planted with potatoes (often used to make Golden Wonder crisps) which gave rise to its name, chosen by local schoolchildren.

Walk forward and, after a gate, turn left roughly parellel with the canal to a stile and Burford Lane. Then turn right and walk uphill to a footpath sign on your right.

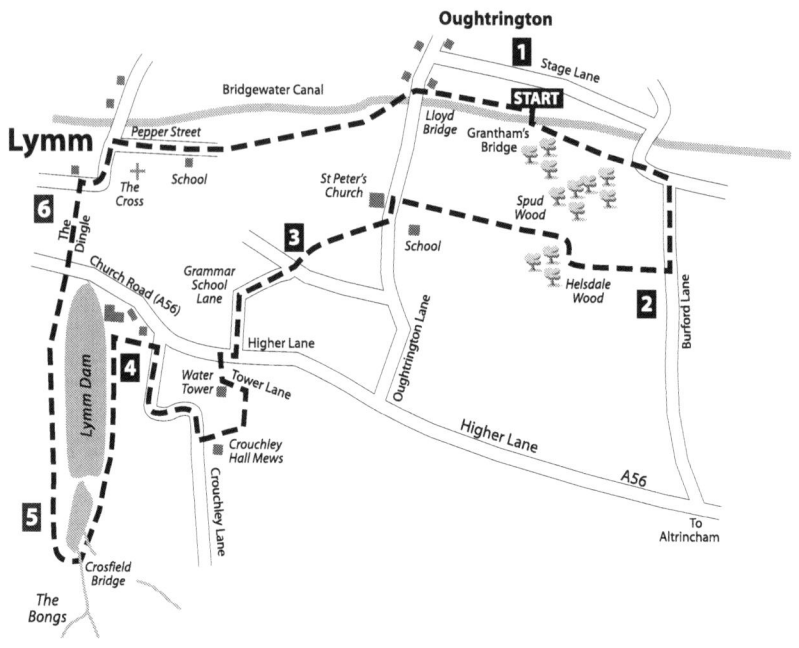

2. Go through the gap here and walk ahead with the hedge on your left. Turn right before the pond at the field's end, then go left through the gap into Helsdale Wood. Keep ahead through this pretty woodland, then continue forward again alongside fields.

Passing Lymm High School's playing fields you can see how the school's Elizabethan mansion has been dwarfed by new buildings.

On reaching Oughtrington Lane turn left to pass St Peter's parish church before going right along a footpath.

This church was built in Gothic style in 1874 at a cost of £10,000, all paid for by George Dewhurst, a local cotton manufacturer. The stone for its structure came from a quarry in Helsdale Wood and all the woodwork inside is of oak, except for the pews which are deal – cotton manufacturing hitting a bad patch at that time.

3. Ignore the sharp right turn at the end onto Longbutt Lane, which possibly formed the original boundary between Lymm and Oughtrington. Instead, keep straight ahead along Grammar

School Road which bends up to the A56 (Higher Lane). Cross this with extreme care and turn right, then left down Tower Lane and, at its end, keep ahead down a gravel footpath.

The water tower here was much in the news when being converted into a state-of-the-art family home.

At a field turn left along its side for a short distance, then go right down a grassy track. This continues between hawthorn hedges before veering right to pass behind the attractive barn conversions of Crouchley Hall Mews (renovated in 1996). Turn right at Crouchley Lane and walk almost to the A56 before turning left through the church hall car park to reach Lymm Dam.

Lymm Dam was formed early in the 19th century when the village needed extra water to power new industrial machinery. Today it is a local beauty spot. Great crested grebe breed on it; fishermen hope to catch carp or pike and, at dusk, pipistrelle bats flit in the trees.

The tower of St Mary's church, Lymm, reflected in the tranquil waters of Lymm Dam

4. Turn left along the lakeside path to Crosfield Bridge.

This imposing structure was built by Lord Leverhulme in 1918. He also planted the Lombardy poplars but his plans for a housing development in the area were never realised.

5. Cross the bridge and perhaps make a detour down the path on your left to visit The Bongs.

Three ponds have been restored in this area and thuggish rhododendron and other non-native species have been cleared to allow wildflowers to flourish. Kingcups and flag iris enjoy the wetland; bluebells (whitebells too), ramsons, celandines and wood anemone are prolific in the woodland; meadow cranesbill and meadowsweet thrive in the more open areas. You may even hear a woodpecker tapping away on a tree trunk or see the orange and blue flash of a kingfisher as it streaks over the water.

Then turn back along this side of the lake to arrive at Church Road (A56) which was built at the same time as Lymm Dam as a turnpike road from Warrington to Stockport.

A place of worship has stood on the rising ground here since the 10th century and St Mary's church was rebuilt in 1851 with financial help from the Dewhursts. Living in Lymm at the time, this wealthy cotton family also built St Peter's church in Oughtrington.

Cross this busy road with care and continue forward down steps into The Dingle. This gorge, with walls 100 feet/30 metres high, drops down to the weir and the village.

Look up the road to your left and you will see The Spread Eagle, with its inn sign of a large brass bird. Lymm is well-endowed with inns – five in the village itself and several more on the outskirts. The settlement was built on a rock and around here you can see how both streets and houses have been cut out of the rock face.

6. Turn right to Lymm Cross.

This is one of the best examples of a village cross still in existence. It stands on a weathered flight of sandstone steps and rumour has it that St Paul preached from them. Certainly, it used to act as a rostrum for both preachers and speakers. Above the steps each sundial has a different inscription on it. The village stocks, erected in 1775, stand nearby, once used to sober up those who had drunk too much.

Cock fighting also used to take place in the square and Lymm may have been the last place in England where this cruel pastime was abolished. An old Cheshire rhyme refers to the colours of the game cocks bred in this area for sport.

"Lymon Greys, Statham Blacks,
Warburton Blue and Peover Pecks." *(speckled)*

You may wish to spend more time in this pretty village before leaving The Cross along Pepper Street.

The first part of this road is cobbled and is thought to date from Roman times. Its name perhaps dates from medieval times when spices could be bought from a market here to flavour food.

After passing Ravenbank primary school, keep straight ahead down the footpath. The tall spire of St Peter's church soon comes into view – a soaring local landmark.

7. At Oughtrington Lane turn left over Lloyd Bridge.

Originally called Dog Bridge as the Dog Inn stood nearby, it was renamed after a local family who worked on the canal for 200 years.

Drop down onto the towpath of the Bridgewater Canal. Turn left along it back to Grantham's Bridge and the walk's end.

6. Preston-on-the-Hill

Lewis Carroll's birthplace and the millennium woodland commemorating his centenary

Morphany Lane, Summer Lane, New Manor Farm, Higher Lane, Lewis Carroll Wood

Start: *Morphany Lane. Map reference: SJ 595804.*

By Car: *Leave Warrington on the A49. Cross over the M56, then take the second turn right down Grimsditch Lane. Keep left into Higher Lane and, after passing Brook House Farm, park in the layby just after the junction with Morphany Lane.*

Distance: *3 miles/5 kilometres.*

Duration: *Allow 1 to 2 hours.*

Difficulty: *Easy. On a clear day this is a bright breezy walk, over fields and along country lanes.*

Food and Drink: *None.*

Map: *OS 1:25,000 Explorer 267 Northwich & Delamere Forest.*

The walk

1. Turn left up Morphany Lane and immediately take the path to the site of Lewis Carroll's birthplace – a magical well-maintained place of pilgrimage for many.

The memorial stone, which used to stand by the roadside, faces you as you reach the site. On it you can read the verse from his poem, Three Sunsets, *in which he refers to this delightful place.*

> "An island farm, midst seas of corn,
> Swayed by the wandering breath of morn,
> The happy spot where I was born ..."

The parsonage was burnt down in 1883 but its footprint is traceable on the ground and an information board has a plan of the rooms. Another

Preston-on-the-Hill

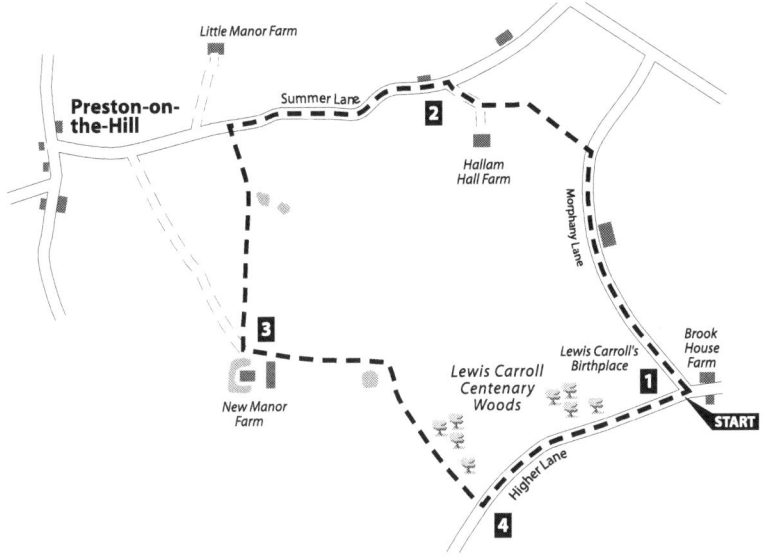

board gives details of Lewis Carroll's life. And don't miss the dormouse depicted on the iron cover over the well.

Continue up oak-lined Morphany Lane, passing Morphany Old Hall East and West, before turning left down a footpath, signposted to Summer Lane. Cross the bridge here and go through a kissing gate, then follow the ridge up the side of two fields to arrive at the road leading to Hallam Hall and its converted barns. Turn right along this road and you soon reach Summer Lane.

2. Turn left, passing pretty cottages and continue down to a footpath sign on the left. Climb over the stile here and walk ahead with the hedge on your right. Cross the ditch at the bottom of this field, climb over a rickety stile and keep forward again down the side of the next field. Negotiate another stile and walk across the next field to a stile in the facing hedge, after which you turn left along the road to New Manor Farm.

3. The farmhouse is moated – a feature of many early Cheshire farms, designed more to keep out local burglars rather than an army. Do not go right through the arch to the main farm buildings but turn left over a stile before an attractive converted brick barn.

Continue with the hedge on your right until you join a track and pass a small copse. Bear right over the stile here and, keeping the fence on your right, continue to the stile at the corner of a wood. Walk ahead down the side of this, then go straight across the field to a stile in the facing hedge. Cross the next small field to another stile, then turn left along Higher Lane.

4. Continue until you come to the Lewis Carroll Centenary Wood on your left which is worth a visit.

To celebrate the Millennium this was planted by the Woodland Trust, with a mixture of oak, ash, wild cherry, rowan and hazel. A small pond is also home to smooth newts, frogs and dragonflies. And don't miss the Lewis Carroll centenary feature — a hexagon of six oaks which echo the author's fascination with mathematics. It's a peaceful spot.

It is then only a short distance along Higher Lane back to your car and the birthplace of Lewis Carroll – a perfect picnic spot.

A memorial stone marks the site of Lewis Carroll's birthplace.

7. Thelwall

Two canals and a penny ferry

Weaste Lane, Bridgewater Canal, Dean's Lane, Laskey Lane, Thelwall village, Penny Ferry, Gig Lane, Pickering Bridge

Start: *Cliff Road, Thelwall. Map reference: SJ 647863.*

By Car: *Take the A50 south from Warrington. Continue ahead at the A56 traffic lights towards the M6, then turn left immediately into Cliff Road – signposted to Massey Brook. Drive under the underpass and park at the far end of the road, before it rejoins the A50.*

Distance: *4 miles/6.5 kilometres*

Duration: *Allow 2 hours.*

Difficulty: *Easy, on canal towpath, lanes and field footpaths.*

Food and Drink: *Pickering Arms in Thelwall (01925 261001). Attractive, atmospheric, friendly pub.*

Map: *OS 1:25,000 Explorer 276 Bolton, Wigan & Warrington*

The walk

1. Walk forward to the main road and turn left along it. After passing kennels turn left at the end of the next field, walking down a rough track which, at the far end, becomes a narrow footpath between houses that leads to Weaste Lane.

Turn right and almost immediately left down another footpath. Follow this down the field, then over the Bridgewater Canal on Pickering's Bridge – named after a Lord of the Manor who settled here in 1662. Drop down to the towpath and turn left along it towards Lymm, walking past boats moored along the far bank.

2. As you pass Thelwall Underbridge, which takes Halfacre Lane under the canal, you come to a small wood – a delightful spot. After this turn left along Dean's Wharf, through an attractive

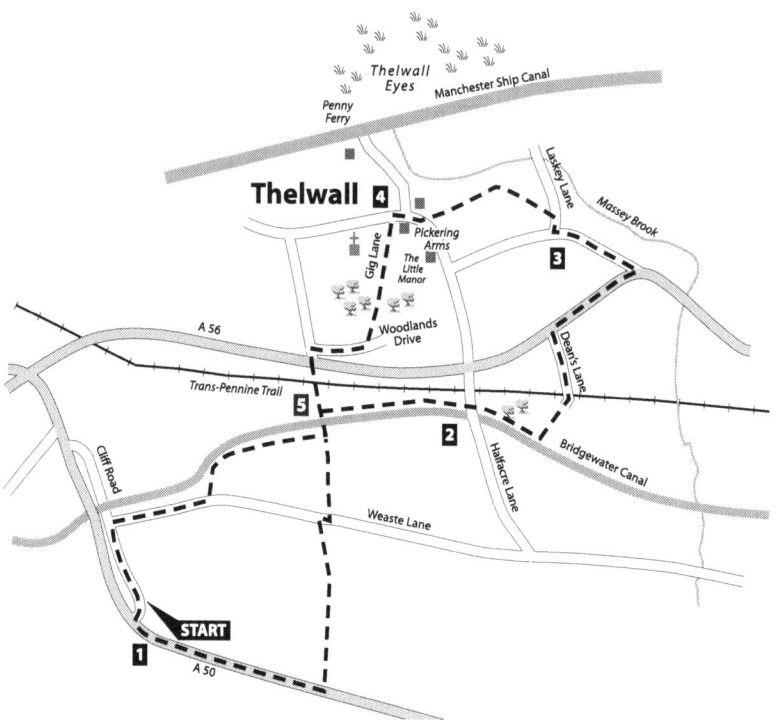

modern housing estate which takes you to a bridge over the disused railway.

Today this is part of the Trans-Pennine Trail which runs from Southport to Hornsea. The stretch here follows the defunct Timperley to Garstang railway. This line reached Lymm in 1853, its embankments having been built using sandstone excavated from the Manchester Ship Canal. Passenger services then operated for just over 100 years.

Turn right when you reach the A56 and cross over with care. Look out for the old iron signpost set into the hedge of Number 515 before turning left along the old Lymm Road.

From here you have an excellent view of the Thelwall viaduct which takes the M6 over the Manchester Ship Canal. All the Cheshire section of the M6 was completed in 1963 but the viaduct has been considerably widened since then.

You soon come to stables. Falconry used to be a popular pastime at Old Hall Farm here, the birds roosting in the house's rafters.

3. Turn right into Laskey Lane and immediately left down a narrow footpath. After going through a small gate, cross the field in the same direction, making for the new sports hall of Chaigeley School. Behind this the path then continues ahead through woodland beside a brick wall – the school's boundary. Near the far end a culvert of clear water runs out from under the wall and drops down to Massey Brook over paving stones.

The River Mersey has been straightened and deepened for boats since the 17th century. Then, in the 1880s the Manchester Ship Canal cut off the remaining old loops. The stream here flows in the old river bed.

4. The path comes out at what was Thelwall post office.

Opposite is the Pickering Arms. An ancient tavern, dating from the 16th century, the writing on its gable end is translated from an Anglo-Saxon Chronicle which states:

IN THE YEAR 923

KING EDWARD THE ELDER FOUNDED A CYTY HERE

AND CALLED IT THELWALL

Before the cutting of the Manchester Ship Canal the houses round here were subject to flooding and enough water is once reputed to have collected in the cellars of the Pickering Arms to put out a fire in the bakery attached to the post office opposite. Another source tells how a pig trough was used as a raft by the bakery to deliver the bread.

For a short detour to an idyllic picnic spot, turn right down Ferry Lane, passing the attractive sandstone Thelwall Old Hall, before the track bends left to the 'penny ferry'.

This still operates, taking foot passengers across the Manchester Ship Canal to the nature reserve of Thelwall Eyes. Originally marshland, this, and Woolston Eyes, were raised by dredgings when the Manchester Ship Canal was built, so that today they form a wet plateau of reeds, rough grass and scrub – ideal habitats for many birds and mammals.

Return to the Pickering Arms and turn right.

Lettering carved into the gable end of the Pickering Arms at Thelwall reminds us that this was once a Saxon city

Ahead is All Saints Church. Built in 1843, all its windows are of stained glass. One is dedicated to the memory of Sir Peter Rylands and his wife, and it shows the Rylands' family crest and a wiredrawer at his bench. Thanks to his far-sightedness and hard work, in the 1950s his company was the leading wire manufacturer in Great Britain.

However, before reaching the church turn left into Gig Lane, passing the old village school then soon reaching an attractive park. After passing the back of The Little Manor bear right at a junction to cross this, then leave it by a passage flanked by ornamental walls. On reaching a road (Woodlands Drive) turn right and, at its end, turn left to cross the main road (A56) with care and go down the track opposite.

5. Cross the disused railway and the canal, then turn right alongside this. The path meanders along the bank until you turn left up to Weaste Lane. Turn right along here, then left at its end up Cliff Road and back to your car.

8. Brown Knowl
Ancient fort and far-reaching views
Larkton Hill, Maiden Castle, Sandstone Trail, Bickerton Hill

Start: *Brown Knowl. Map reference: SJ 497536.*

By Car: *Take the A41 south from Chester, then turn left onto the A534. (Once known as the Salters Way, this was the route from Nantwich to Chester taken by salt traders.) Turn right into Brown Knowl village. Park in the vicinity of the telephone box (Now a defibrillator box). Alternatively, you may wish to turn left here and park in Reading Room Lane.*

Distance: *3 miles/5 kilometres.*

Duration: *Allow 1 to 2 hours.*

Difficulty: *One climb up onto Larkton Hill.*

Food and Drink: *Egerton Arms, Broxton (01829 782241).*

Map: *OS 1:25,000 Explorer 257 Crewe & Nantwich.*

The walk

1. Walk uphill past the Methodist chapel and take the left fork down Lower Sandy Lane – a 'No Through Road'. At the T-junction turn right, then left at the house ahead. Continue past Tanglewood, noting the carved inscription on a stone gatepost, then take the left fork to Bickerton Hill where you enter land owned by the National Trust.

This is one of the few remaining heathlands in Cheshire. In July bilberry pickers may be seen crouched low, combing the bushes for these tiny, hidden fruit.

Go straight ahead past an information board and through a footgate, climbing up on a sandy path until, at a clearing, you turn left uphill past a waymarker post banning horse riders. Continue, climbing gently through heather, bilberries, bracken and silver birch, perhaps pausing to enjoy the outstanding views

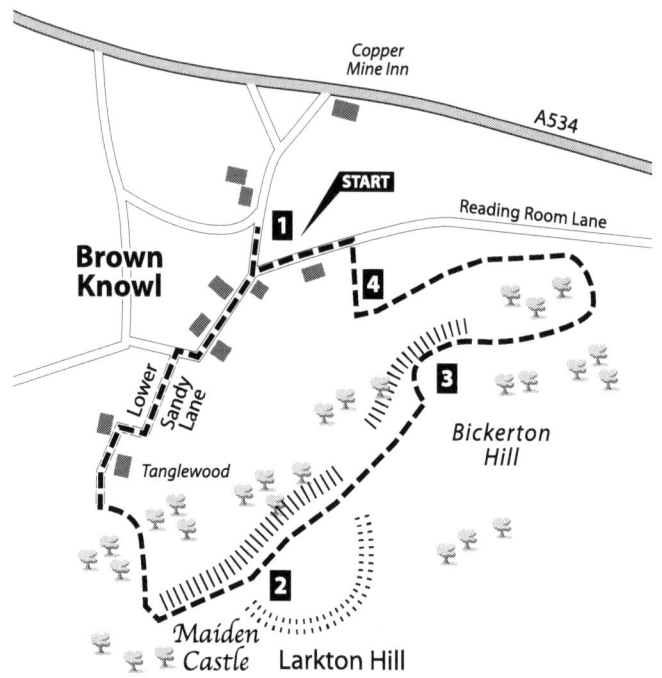

over to the Welsh hills. From the top of the hill, drop down into a valley to join the Sandstone Trail at a junction of paths. Follow this – signposted to 'Maiden Castle' – up rough-hewn steps to the hillfort and a tree-trunk seat.

Occupied some 2,000 years ago, this Iron Age fort consisted of two stone and earth ramparts, each with an external ditch. The cliff then formed the western edge of the settlement which had a single entrance of inturned defensive banks. Today, mounds of earth are the only evidence of its existence.

The ancient word maegden *means 'untaken fort' and the folk living here would have been farmers and hunters, who perhaps also traded in salt and pottery. Their homes would have been circular, probably built of wattle and daub with thatched roofs.*

2. Follow Sandstone Trail markers in a north-easterly direction along the lip of Bickerton Hill, then through woodland.

The level of noise can vary enormously, from the loud whistling of the wind as you walk along the exposed ridge, to a haven of quiet as you move into the wood's shelter. You may notice parasitic witch's broom on the silver birch; and look out for fungi in autumn.

3. Eventually drop down steps to a junction of sandy tracks. Keep ahead here and the path soon curves uphill again to the left to reach the superb panorama at Kitty's Stone.

Bilberries and heather spread out from the path and you pass a sandstone block inscribed with poems by Leslie Wheeldon in memory of his wife Kitty (née Scott) – a monument known locally as Kitty's Stone.

Continue along the crest, then into woodland and down stone steps. When the path forks halfway down the slope, bear left and continue losing height through the trees. At the bottom of the slope, immediately before a kissing gate, leave the Sandstone

Known locally as Kitty's Stone, this sandstone memorial commemorates a lost partner and happy days outdoors

Trail and turn left down the side of a field. At the bottom, bear left along the fence on a National Trust path at the wood's edge. The path then doubles back the way you have come, following the base of the scarp at a lower level.

4. Eventually, go through a kissing gate on your right beside a metal National Trust sign and head down the field boundary to a stile. Notice the ancient beech as you turn left along Reading Room Lane. Then follow this pleasant country lane back into Brown Knowl village.

Looking down to the village of Brown Knowl from Bickerton Hill

9. Bunbury
So much of interest along the way

St Boniface Church, River Gowy, Beeston Market, Shropshire Union Canal, Bunbury Locks, Bunbury Mill

Start: *The green by St Boniface church, Bunbury. Map reference: SJ 570581.*

By Car: *Take the A51 from Nantwich toards Chester. Turn left in Alpraham. As you drive into Bunbury on Bowes Gate Road, park by the green in front of the church.*

Distance: *7 miles/11 kilometres.*

Duration: *Allow 4 hours.*

Difficulty: *Easy.*

Food and Drink: *Dysart Arms in Bunbury (01829 260183); Lockgate Coffee House (01829 730592); Bunbury Mill (01829 733244).*

Map: *OS 1:25,000 Explorer 257 Crewe & Nantwich.*

The walk

1. Walk back to the church and turn right over a stile into the cemetery (on the opposite side of the road to the church). Follow the hedge down to a wooden stile, then veer left across the field to another stile. Turn left up College Lane, pass a converted chapel then go right over a stile just before the next house.

Follow the wall, then the hedge, down the side of the field into a little valley. After going through a metal kissing gate keep to the high ground across the next field until you come to a signpost by a pylon and drop down diagonally to cross the tiny River Gowy.

2. With the fence on your right, walk along to the next kissing gate, then continue through a delightful copse of many native species, including blackthorn, rambling rose, hawthorn, silver

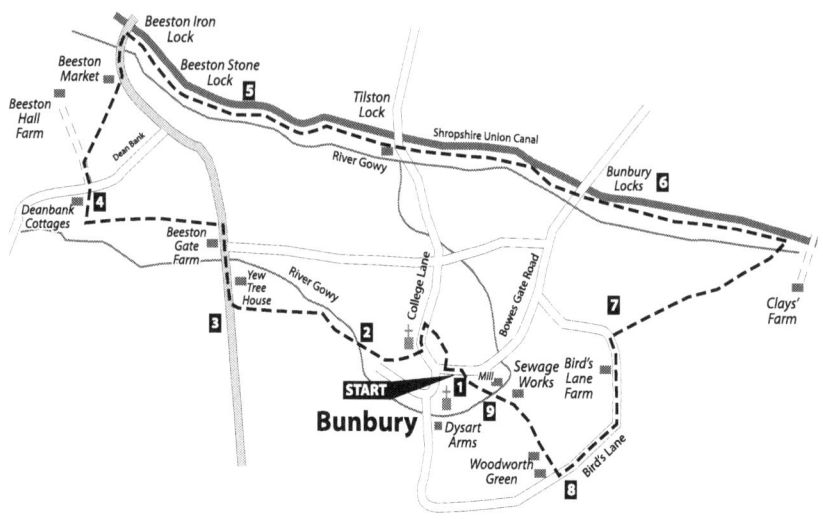

birch, rowan and holly, which you leave via another kissing gate, above which tower much older Scots pine. Immediately, cross a high stile on your right and continue diagonally left over a large ploughed field to reach a footbridge that you don't cross. Instead, turn left, keeping the river on your right as you follow the line of an overgrown hedge to a steel kissing gate. Then, with the fence on your right, walk along the side of the next field, then a much smaller field, to a stile and the A49.

3. Turn right along the footpath here, passing Yew Tree House with its mullioned windows. Then cross this busy road with great care before reaching Beeston Gate Farm. Built in typical Cheshire style, the farmhouse is enhanced by gables and honeycomb windows. Immediately after this turn left through a metal gate with Beeston Castle ahead.

Walk down the right-hand side of this field, then follow signs over several more fields in the same direction until you reach a grassy track which takes you to Deanbank Cottages.

4. Cross the country lane here (Dean Bank) and walk ahead along the tarmac drive of Beeston Hall Farm complex. About half-way along turn right over a stile and drop down a path through a copse mainly comprising silver birch and rowan. Then skirt a field and cross rough ground to the track that used to lead to Beeston cattle market.

The market used to be known as the Smithfield of the North but it ceased trading in 2019. (Construction of a housing estate may necessitate a small diversion here to reach the A49.)

Turn left along the road, walk under the railway bridge, pass the Lockgate Coffee House, cross the River Gowy, then drop down to the towpath of the Shropshire Union canal. Turning right to walk under the stone bridge you immediately arrive at Beeston Iron Lock – a pleasant picnic spot.

This section of the canal was completed in 1779 but the running sand found in this area caused problems, with banks caving in and, in 1787, the original lock itself collapsed.

In 1813 the canal had new owners and new engineers (Thomas Denton and Thomas Telford) and both the Beeston locks were rebuilt, the top lock still of stone but this lower one of iron plate, using the successful method developed by William Jessop and Thomas Telford for the famous Pontcysyllte aqueduct in North Wales. The canal was also re-aligned and it finally re-opened in 1828.

5. You will soon pass Beeston Stone Lock.

Notice the small circular building here with chimney and bricked-in window. (There is another at Tilston Lock.) In the canal's heyday the maintenance equipment of lengthsmen responsible for a stretch of canal was stored in these. As you walk along you will also notice the brick shelters housing stop planks for use if the canal bank is breached.

Farther along you come to Tilston Lock.

In a delightful setting, an attractively converted former mill, built in 1838, stands astride the River Gowy here. Notice its ornate drainpipes, eaves and wide, high doorway, from which sacks of flour would be passed onto a cart waiting below.

Manoeuvring the boats into Bunbury Locks proves to be a tricky business

If you are weary, you can cut back to your car, either from here or from Bunbury Locks which are worth seeing.

Continuing along the towpath you next come to an iron railway bridge made at Roodee Foundry, Chester, now much reinforced by brick and concrete. You then reach the staircase locks at Bunbury where a shop sells refreshments.

Notice here the fine stable block, each stall having its own chimney. How warm and welcoming it must have been for the weary horses. At one time fast 'fly-boats' covered the 80 miles from the Mersey estuary to factories in the Midlands in little more than 24 hours, so it was essential to have a change of horse.

6. To complete the walk, continue along the canal, which you leave just before the next bridge. After passing a post provided by the Shropshire Union Canal Society (No. 48H) drop down off the towpath and go through a metal kissing gate. Then cross the field to a plank bridge over the tiny River Gowy. Walk up the field to a kissing gate, then cross to another one.

Follow the line of poles all the way across the next field, where the path may be indistinct, and leave it by way of a stile and a plank by the final gate. Keep well to the right of the poles across the following field to go through a metal kissing gate and negotiate slippery planks in the corner, between an oak and an ash. Then keep the barbed wire fence and hedge on your left as you cross the next field and exit it beside an oak at the far end. Cross the following field diagonally, noting the line of trees along the lost hedge where you dip down. It is another very ridged field and you pass a pond on your left.

7. Finally, cross a stile between a gate and a trough, and turn left along Bird's Lane. After passing attractive Bird's Lane Farm, the sandstone tower of Bunbury Church indicates that you are nearing the end of your walk.

8. When you reach the tiny hamlet of Woodworth Green turn right over a stile immediately before Woodworth Lodge and, at the hedge's end, bear left across the field, making for a gate which lies between an oak and a pylon. Go through this and cross the next field, passing the sewage works on your right before dropping down to a stile. From here cross the board walk to a pretty picnic area and Bunbury Mill.

A mill has existed at Bunbury since 1290 and the present building dates from about 1850. It operated commercially until 1960 when a massive flood ended its working life. At that time Thomas Parker & Son were the millers, and flour was taken by horse and cart to Chester. Walking past the door in the wall of the upper storey you can visualise how sacks full of flour were passed out and loaded onto a cart below.

The mill and its machinery were restored to working order by United Utilities in 1977 and it is normally open to the public on Sundays and Bank Holiday Mondays when you can see it in use, with flour once again on sale. As you descend steps formed by an old millstone read the rhyme on the mill door exhorting the miller to be kind and honest.

9. You have a choice here. Either walk up past the cottages on the old cobbles, then turn left up the road back to the church. Alternatively, go through the gate into the field at the far side of the circular car park, walk up the field towards the church and climb over the corner stile.

St Boniface church is one of the great churches of Cheshire with its west tower dating from early in the 14th century. In the middle of the chancel floor, the tomb of Sir Hugh Calveley has a seven foot long alabaster effigy surrounded by its original spiked iron railing and the octagonal font of 1663 retains its original cover.

10. Grindley Brook

Enjoy canal locks and rural bridleways

Shropshire Union Canal, Bishop Bennet Way, Wirswall, Willey Moor Lock

Start: *Grindley Brook. Map reference: SJ 524429.*

By Car: *Take the A41 from Whitchurch towards Chester. Approaching Grindley Brook, park in the lay-by on the left, in front of the near-derelict mill. If this is full continue to the Horse and Jockey, where you may be allowed to park.*

Distance: *5 miles/8 kilometres.*

Duration: *Allow 2 to 3 hours.*

Difficulty: *Easy. One very muddy section.*

Food and Drink: *Lockside Cafe (01948 663385) and the Horse and Jockey (01948 662723 at Grindley Brook.*
Willey Moor Lock Tavern (01948 663274).

Map: *OS 1:25,000 Explorer 257 Crewe & Nantwich.*

The walk

1. From the lay-by walk forward to the Lockside Cafe and the start of a staircase of three locks, this being the Bottom Lock. Drop down to the Shropshire Union Canal here and turn left, under the road bridge. Continue along the towpath to the next bridge (No. 28), where there is a shop.

Leave the canal here, cross over the bridge and follow the stony track under the obsolete railway and up to Grindley Brook Farm where you turn left in front of the farmhouse. You are now on the Bishop Bennet Way and the South Cheshire Way.

Keep forward with the hedge on your right until you drop downhill and go through a steel gate ahead, ignoring all other paths. A patch of purple autumn-flowering crocuses brighten

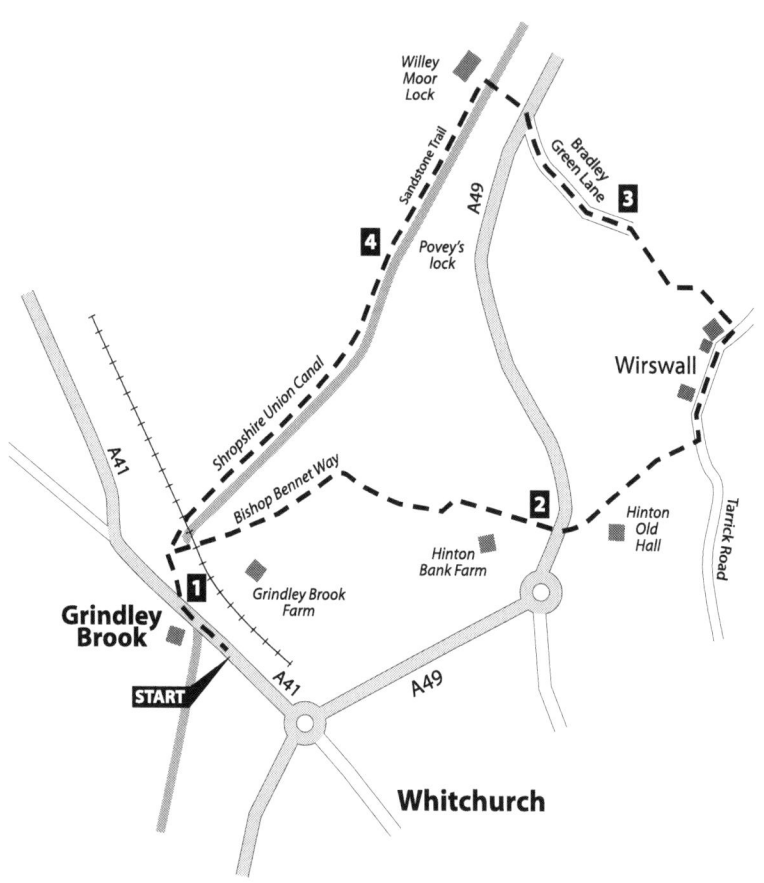

the grass here as you continue forward on a sheltered path. Turn left just before you reach Hinton Bank Farm and walk up the field. Then turn right along a track, crossing a cattle grid and continuing forward to the A49.

2. Cross this with care and walk up the drive (a bridleway) opposite. Go through the gate on the left before you reach the Hinton Old Hall complex and continue past the buildings. Walk

Grindley Brook

in the same direction up the side of a field, where rabbits burrow in the sandy banks, eventually passing between gorse bushes to a stile and a splendid view. From here continue forward along a track all the way to Terrick Road.

Turn left into Wirswall, passing The Grange, Wirswall Hall and The Paddocks before turning left along a bridleway (signposted to The Spinney). Keep left along this track, with views across the Cheshire Plain to the Peckforton Hills. It may be very muddy as you reach a steel gate and continue down a path towards Bradeley Green.

3. Continue forward down Bradeley Green Lane. When you reach the A49 again, cross over and turn right then immediately left over a stile, walking down to Willey Moor Lock, where you cross the canal. (You may prefer to walk down the access road here.)

A busy staircase of three locks at Grindley Brook on the Shropshire Union Canal, north of Whitchurch

Occupying a building dating back to 1700, Willey Moor Lock Tavern was originally a lock-keeper's cottage. At first teas were served as a side-line, then this expanded into serving drinks with meals. Today the premises are fully licensed and it's an idyllic spot in which to watch the boats go by, glass in hand.

4. After turning left along the towpath you soon pass Povey's Lock, walk under bridge No. 26 and continue through a passageway of tall common reeds.

Approaching Grindley Brook, notice the Sandstone Trail milestone (or rather kilometre stone) 51 kms to Frodsham, 4 kms to Whitchurch.

You then walk under Bridge No. 27.

This fine skew bridge of blue engineering bricks is almost long enough to be a tunnel. It carries the trackbed of the old Chester to Whitchurch railway over the canal

To finish, retrace your footsteps along the canal to the Horse and Jockey or the Lockside Cafe where I can recommend the homemade cakes.

Lymm Cross is a rare surviving medieval village cross (Walk 5)

Dawn colours the Shropshire Union Canal near Bunbury (Walk 9)

A single red poppy decorates a field edge in west Cheshire

A narrowboat moored close to black-and-white Acton Bridge (Walk 21)

Anderton Lift is now celebrated as the 'cathedral of the canals' (Walk 16)

Yellow oilseed rape frames a Georgian farmhouse at Alvanley (Walk 22)

Strolling through sun-dappled Delamere Forest (Walk 23)

Cheshire's twin castles: medieval Beeston and Victorian Peckforton (Walk 14)

Traditional narrowboat art on the Cheshire Ring

Panoramic views from the top of Beeston Crag (Walk 12)

Black-and-white 'magpie' architecture at Peckforton (Walk 12)

Rain sweeps across the Cheshire Plain towards Rawhead (Walk 13)

Purple heather and yellow gorse on Cheshire's sandstone hills (Walk 8)

Dramatic cliffs near Muskets Hole on the Sandstone Trail (Walk 13)

Heather and gorse decorate Thurstaston Common (Walk 30)

11. Malpas

Enjoy fields, woodland, sandstone cliffs and some ancient history

Chester Road, Tilston Road, Gam's Wood, Kidnal, Overton Scar, Overton Heath, Twelve Apostles, St Oswald's Church

Start: *Malpas. Map reference: SJ 487473.*

By Car: *Take the A41 from Whitchurch. In Grindley Brook branch left onto the B5395. Pass the cross in the centre of Malpas, then look out for the public car park on the right.*

Distance: *5 miles/8 kilometres.*

Duration: *Allow 2 to 3 hours.*

Difficulty: *Easy. One very muddy section.*

Food and Drink: *The Nisa local shop and the Fire Station cafe are near the car park. Clustering around The Cross in the centre are also Gabbie's Deli (01948 860400) and A Table at Eaton's (01948 861177) which serve light lunches. The Red Lion usually serves food too (01948 860368).*

Map: *OS 1:25,000 Explorer 257 Crewe & Nantwich.*

The walk

1. Walk back up to the High Street and turn right. Then go right again down Chester Road at the post office, heading towards the Bishop Heber High School. Pass the cemetery and Oathills before turning left up Hollowood Road.

At its end continue along the byway – muddy in places. Just before Mates Lane turn left at a long field's end, along a sheltered path between fields. Continue walking in the same direction, keeping to the edge of fields all the way to Tilston Road.

Its very straightness indicates its Roman origin, when it was the main route between Deva *(Chester) and* Mediolanum *(Whitchurch).*

Fourteenth-century St Oswald's church at Malpas occupies a low hill alongside the remains of a Norman motte and bailey castle

In fact Malpas—one of Cheshire's oldest settlements—was set up at that time as an outpost for travellers.

2. Turn right along this and, at the first bend, keep straight ahead down another byway – a muddy track which drops down through Gam's Wood between hugh sandstone cliffs. Reaching the road again, turn left to the hamlet of Kidnal, passing Kidnal Grange before turning left down Whitewood Lane opposite Kidnal House.

At the first corner turn left past black security gates onto a gravel track, leaving this when it winds uphill. After going through a metal gate continue on a sheltered path alongside fields and below the rocky outcrops of the well wooded Overton Scar. Wonderful westerly views open up all along here.

3. Continue alongside the wood until eventually you reach a track, where caves are gouged out beneath huge cliff overhangs. Continue forward past these on the track – part of the Marches' Way and the Bishop Bennet Way – to Overton Hall. From here continue along a muddy track to a steel gate and horse gate. You can then enjoy a sheltered path between tall trees, which is much better underfoot and leads to a lane.

4. Bear right along this and ignore the byway to Cuddington Heath on the right. After passing Overton Lodge and stables climb halfway up the hill, then turn right up steep steps to a steel kissing gate. Cross the field to another kissing gate by a huge sycamore – still on the Marches' Way – and keep ahead past a line of trees.

Twelve sycamores were planted here, symbolising the twelve apostles, and when one dies or becomes diseased it is replaced.

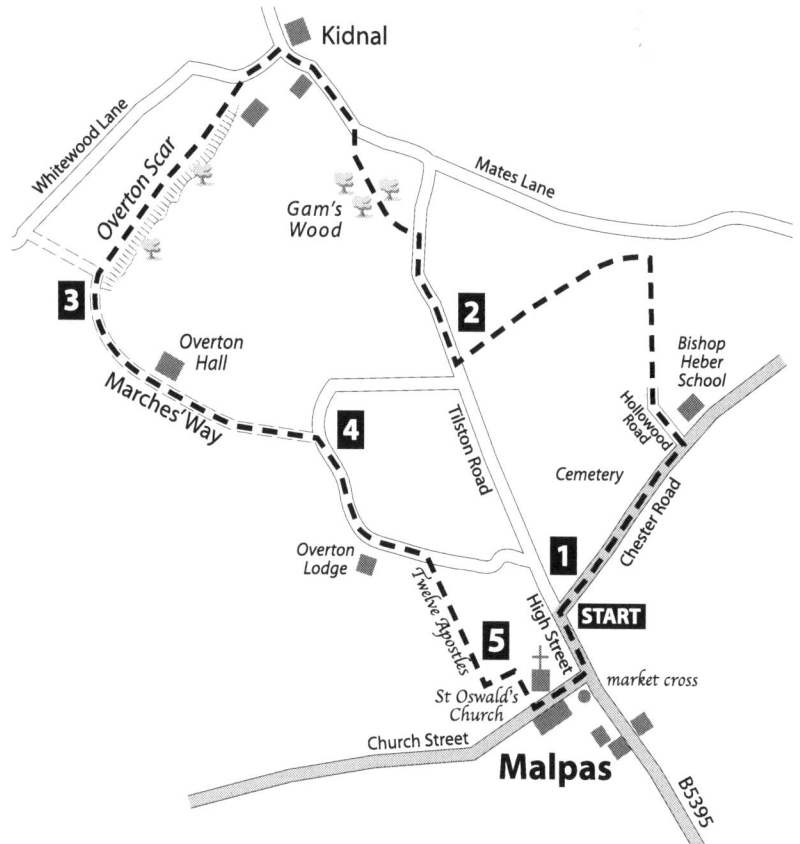

5. Passing a wood you come to a wooden kissing gate on the left and a concrete drive. Then bear left by a deserted building to the church.

Behind this is a huge, high mound – the remains of a motte and bailey castle, built in Norman times as protection from Welsh raids.

The church is well worth a visit. Dedicated to St Oswald it originates from the 14th century and is an imposing building, with a massive tower and a great array of gargoyles on its outer walls. The interior boasts many splendid features including the nave's glorious ceiling and a 13th century chest seven feet long, its intricate ironwork crafted by a local blacksmith. Ornate 16th century screens lead into side chapels dedicated to the Cholmondeley and Brereton families, which contain magnificent monuments.

There is also Flemish stained glass to admire and the glorious east window is dedicated to Reginald Heber. Born in the tower of the rectory here, he became a parson like his father and grandfather, and spent the last years of his life in India as Bishop of Calcutta. He was also a great hymn writer. His 'Holy, holy, holy, Lord God Almighty' *is still sung in many churches today and* 'From Greenland's icy mountains, from India's coral strand' *perhaps best epitomises his ministry.*

You leave the church by a handsome two-storey porch, its upper room once housing a priest. The splendid 18th century entrance gates came from Oulton Hall, near Little Budworth.

Turn left along Church Street to the market square.

On the way you will pass the Market House. Fronted by a colonnade of eight Tuscan pillars, it was built by the Drake family in 1762 as a shop with living accommodation above.

Only the sandstone steps remain of the medieval market cross which was removed in the 19th century. Today's ornate replacement was erected as a memorial to Charles Thurlow, a Rector of Malpas from 1840 until 1873.

Turn left up the High Street, then right into the car park.

12. Peckforton
Castles ancient and modern, haunted bridge and half-timbered cottages

Beeston Castle, Sandstone Trail, Peckforton Woods, Stone House Lane, Willis's Wood, Beeston village

Start: *Sandstone Trail notice board at Beeston Castle. Map reference: SJ 540590.*

By Car: *Take the A51 from Chester. Turn right at the A49 and follow the signs to Beeston Castle. Beeston Castle is well worth a visit. The 'pay and display' car park opposite the entrance is open from 8am - 6pm, when the gates are locked.*

Distance: *4 miles/6.5 kilometres.*

Duration: *Allow 2 hours.*

Difficulty: *Easy-medium. One short stretch uphill.*

Food and Drink: *Castle Snacks, by the castle, is open. The Pheasant Inn in Higher Burwardsley (01829 770434) requires a small detour.*

Map: *OS 1:25,000 Explorer 257 Crewe & Nantwich.*

The walk

1. Turn left at the castle's entrance and walk to the Sandstone Trail information board and snack bar.

With its jagged precipice rising 300 feet/90 metres above the surrounding countryside, Beeston Crag provided an ideal position for a fortress. In the courtyard, there was also a never-failing supply of fresh water from a well 370 feet/112 metres deep, which is reputed to have treasure buried at its base. So Beeston Castle was built here in 1220 as a military stronghold and has a turbulent history.

You are following the Sandstone Trail for all the first part of this walk. Start by going down the snicket here, following the

Walks in West Cheshire and Wirral

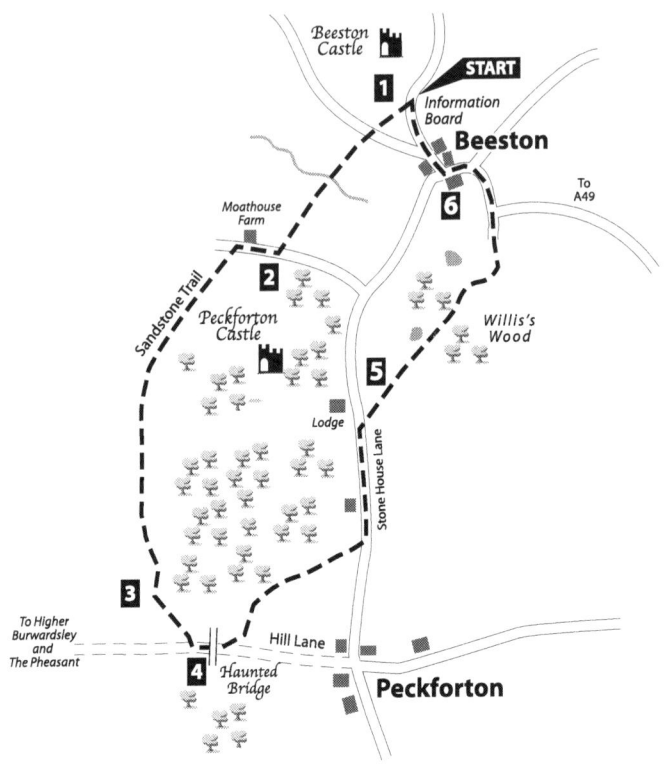

wall for a short way before bearing left down through the wood on a soft carpet of pine needles to the road.

Cross over and bear left and right to a path opposite, signposted to Burwardsley, which unfolds ahead across a field. You eventually drop down to a steel kissing gate and a bridge over a stream, then ascend steps and continue across another field to Horsley Lane. Turn right along this, passing the attractive Moathouse complex with its rough-hewn sandstone buildings, then The Moathouse itself.

Dwarfed by its massive brick chimney, this was originally an Elizabethan farmhouse and a mineral spring noted for the purity of its water surfaces in its grounds.

2. After passing Ivy Cottage turn left into Peckforton Woods, signposted to Burwardsley and Bulkeley Hill. (Look back here for a splendid view of Beeston Castle, high on its hilltop.)

Forestry and pheasant rearing still take place on the estate and these birds may strut across the path. It is a peaceful place, where the wind soughs through the branches. Glimpses of nearby fields appear where the trees thin out and views of the Welsh hills open up.

At the first junction continue ahead towards Burwardsley. Higher Burwardsley lies over to your right, its well-known inn, The Pheasant, often causing walkers to deviate awhile. In the distance the craggy, sandstone cliffs of Rawhead can be seen.

3. Where the track drops down to the right turn left up a narrow path, following the Sandstone Trail towards Bulkeley Hill as the

Beeston Castle towers above the roofline of an Elizabethan farmhouse on Horsley Lane, near Peckforton

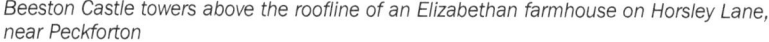

path climbs diagonally up the hillside. Go through the kissing gate at the summit and your way leaves the Sandstone Trail, veering left towards Hill Lane and traversing an area of silver birch and gorse, which can be boggy. At a track, turn left, then left again on reaching Hill Lane to walk under the Haunted Bridge.

This was built in the 1850s to take carriages from Peckforton Castle to the gatehouse. A ghostly servant woman is said to walk from the ruins of a stone hut along the sandy track and up the bank, her severed head under her arm. Local folklore says that if you see her you will die within a year. Cheerful thought!

4. After this, turn left just after the barrier and immediately turn right up the bank at a signpost along a hidden pathway.

Following the Sandstone Trail between the castles of Beeston and Peckforton

This runs parallel with the roadway for a short distance before dropping diagonally down through a rough area, then across a huge field and through a copse to reach Stone House Lane via steep sandstone steps.

For a short detour to see the curious carved sandstone 'Peckforton Elephant' featured on the cover, turn right along the lane here. The statue stands in the front garden of Laundry Cottage, on the right, just past the start of Hill Lane.

Otherwise, turn left along Stone House Lane, eventually passing attractive black-and-white Garden Cottage on the left, with its diamond-paned windows, sandstone stables and cobbled drive. Just before you reach the lodge of Peckforton Castle, fronted by its ancient oak, turn right towards Beeston Moss and Bunbury through a kissing gate. Then veer left along the side of this huge field, only two trees now remaining of the hedgerow that once divided it.

Beeston and Peckforton castles stand aloft on their respective hills. While Beeston Castle is authentically medieval, Peckforton Castle is really a sham. Built by Lord Tollemache in the mid-19th century from locally-quarried sandstone, it was modelled on a Norman castle and was to be his country seat.

5. Turn left at the field's far end until you reach a pleasant path on the right which takes you all the way through Willis's Wood. At the far end bear left at a junction and immediately go right over a stile into a field. Walk alongside a pool, then go straight across the next field to a stile by a gate. Go forward to Moss Lane and turn left.

Brook Farm Cottage, built on a cruck (curved) frame, has been extensively and attractively renovated. Most of the cottages in Beeston date from the 17th century and there are numerous examples of Cheshire's typical 'magpie' dwellings in this area.

6. Turn left at Beeston Old Farm down to Smithy Corner, where a Victorian letter box can be spied in the wall of picturesque Smithy Cottage. Bear right here, then right again past an attractive converted chapel back to the castle.

13. Rawhead

Glorious views from the highest point on the Sandstone Trail.

Gallantry Bank, Tower Wood, Rawhead, Coppermine Lane, Bulkeley Hill

Start: *The old chimney above Gallantry Bank. Map reference: SJ 518542.*

By Car: *Take the A41 south from Chester and turn left onto the A534. After going up Gallantry Bank and passing Gallantry Bank Cottage, park on the right in the lay-by opposite the tall chimney.*

Distance: *4 miles/6.5 kilometres.*

Duration: *Allow 2 hours.*

Difficulty: *Medium. The path rises up to Rawhead and on to Bulkeley Hill.*

Food and Drink: *The Bickerton Poacher (01829 720226) is farther along the A534. The Pheasant Inn (01829 770434) requires a short detour to Higher Burwardsley.*

Map: *OS 1:25,000 Explorer 257 Crewe & Nantwich.*

The walk

1. Cross the road and set off up Coppermine Lane – a 'No Through Road'.

The tall chimney belonged to the pumping house of a copper mine that operated here in the 18th century. Alas, there was not enough copper found to make it economically viable.

At the first corner turn left at a signpost.

Notice the cave set back into the hillside here. There are many stories about the caves in this area – thought to have been hideouts for bands of robbers and highwaymen.

Keep along the fence, which can also be reached by walking through the field past the chimney. Cross the stream then continue up the hill.

Young pheasants may be running in and out of the hedges on their skinny legs here and as you skirt Tower Wood where they are bred.

2. Turn right onto the Sandstone Trail at the edge of Tower Wood. The signpost points to Rawhead and Beeston and, as the path follows the edge of the wood, the view gets better as you climb higher. Keep straight on after passing Chiflik Farm, which dates from 1875. Bulkeley Hill is then visible over to the right, which you visit on the second part of the walk.

You eventually pass signs warning of the cliff's edge before reaching the deep gully of Muskets Hole where a huge bastion of sandstone faces you. Notice the honeycomb effect of wind erosion on the layers of rock as the path works its way round the head of this gully and up rough-hewn steps.

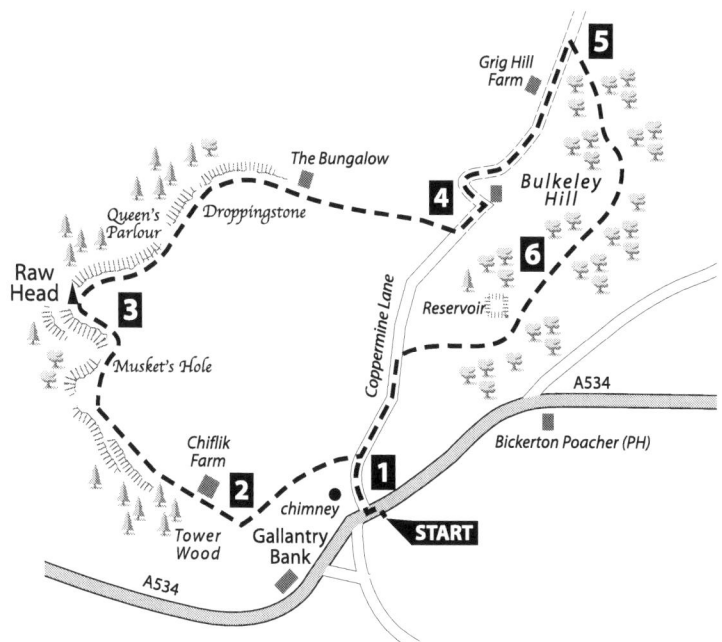

The trig point at Rawhead comes into sight. The highest point on the Sandstone Trail at 746 feet/227 metres above sea level, it is well worth stopping here to admire the outstanding views, which stretch over the Cheshire Plain as far as the Welsh hills. Sandstone slabs also form ideal picnic spots, either here or further along the ridge.

3. Keep along the Sandstone Trail on the top path, which goes along the edge of the scarp by the field's fence.

A spectacular sandstone cave called the Queen's Parlour lies below the path along here. Now hard to find, it is a scramble down to it and is thought to be the result of local men excavating for sand.

The smoothly wooded slopes of Burwardsley Hill can be seen ahead and both Beeston and Peckforton Castles are clearly

Looking out from a viewpoint on the Sandstone Trail to the wooded sandstone cliffs below Rawhead

visible. Descend well-made wooden steps, then continue to a gently dripping rock overhang.

This is where a spring surfaces and is known locally as the Droppingstone – but Drippingstone would be a better description.

Some time after this you go through a kissing gate and turn right. After passing The Bungalow continue ahead to a T-junction and Coppermine Lane again. (Turning right here would be a short-cut back to your car.)

4. However, for the full walk you leave the Sandstone Trail for a while, turning left towards the Peckforton Gap, signposted to Burwardsley. Stay on this track, soon walking between huge gorse bushes. Then, shortly after passing Grig Hill Farm – the second property on the left – turn right at a handrail, up sandstone steps, and rejoin the Sandstone Trail.

5. You are now going up onto Bulkeley Hill—a magical woodland. Climb the steps and the path winds to the right.

The landscape here is composed of silver birch above bracken, heather and bilberry. As you gain height, north-easterly views open up in winter and weirdly-shaped sweet chestnuts crown the crest. Many of these offer ideal climbing opportunities and flat rocks provide platforms from which to view Bulkeley village far below.

6. At last you reach a huge flattish area full of oak trees and, on your left, a narrow, one-track tramway drops steeply downhill.

This was built to transport heavy materials when a water pipeline was being constructed to tap the reservoirs on the summit. Here rainwater percolating through porous sandstone collected on reaching a layer of non-porous clay. These reservoirs provide enough water to supply the villages of south-west Cheshire.

Continue on the Sandstone Trail path along the edge of the escarpment, leaving Bulkeley Hill Wood by a gap in a wire fence. On your right is one of the reservoirs mentioned earlier. From here drop down through Scots pine until you leave the wood by a kissing gate and continue straight on to reach Coppermine Lane, where you turn left and wind downhill back to your car.

14. Tarporley
Rolling fields, a canal and the Sandstone Trail

St Helen's Church, Birch Heath, Pudding Lane, Shropshire Union Canal, Huxley Lane, Sandstone Trail, Tarporley

> **Start:** *Public car park at the southern end of Tarporley. Map reference: SJ 554623.*
>
> **By Car:** *Take the A51 from Chester. On reaching the Tarporley by-pass go ahead to the town. After passing St Helen's church look for signs to the free public car park behind the Community Centre.*
>
> **Distance:** *6 miles/10 kilometres*
>
> **Duration:** *Allow 3 hours.*
>
> **Difficulty:** *Easy.*
>
> **Food and Drink:** *Shady Oak (01829 733159); plenty of eating places in Tarporley including the Swan Hotel (01829 733838) and the Rising Sun (01829 732423)*
>
> **Map:** *OS 1:25,000 Explorer 267 Northwich & Delamere Forest.*

The walk

1. Walk back up the main street, passing the Baptist chapel shared with the Methodists, then the manor house, side-on to the road.

This modest building, said to be the smallest manor house in the country, was built in 1586 by Ralph Done, a prominent local landowner, and the family's coat of arms can still be seen below one of its half-timbered eaves.

Immediately after this, turn left to the lychgate of St Helen's church, where you bear left again down a footpath alongside the churchyard, signposted to Redhill. There are small iron gates at both ends of this path.

Leave the churchyard behind and go ahead across the field to the remains of a stile by an electric fence. Continue straight on to another stile in the hedge on your left, overhung by a hawthorn tree. After this, turn right and soon climb over another stile to reach the bypass.

2. Cross this with great care and continue along the side of the field. At the hedge's end go left over another stile, then turn right to continue in the same direction beside the hedge and heading towards a communications' mast.

You suddenly have a superb view of Beeston Castle and the hills beyond as they roll away in a series of scarps and dips. And looking back, the church and town of Tarporley are framed by trees.

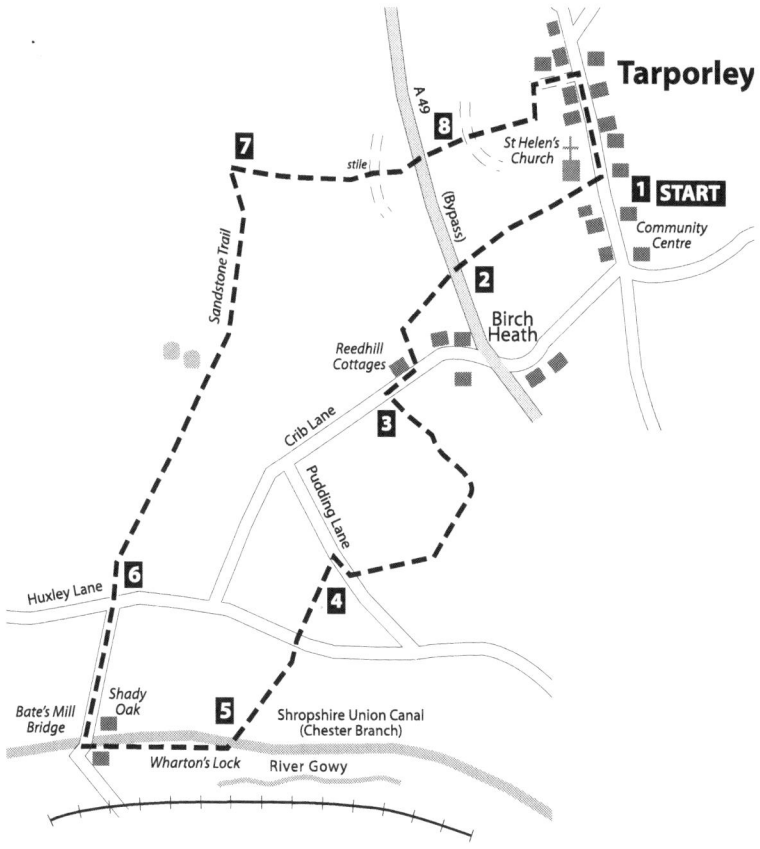

The Done family's coat-of-arms on Tarporley's tiny manor house

Leave the hedge at the mast and continue across the field to two wooden stiles. Then follow a slatted concrete track with the hedge on your left before leaving the field by a metal kissing gate and turning right along Crib Lane past Reedhill Cottages.

3. Soon after this, turn left through a small metal kissing gate beside a copse near a water treatment plant. Turn left and continue along the edge of three fields. Where the hedge makes a right-angled turn in the fourth field **do not go straight on** but bear right to follow it, then cross to a pylon and a stile in the hedge beyond.

The land around Tarporley is ideal for dairy farming and many of the small irregular fields found in this region have been enclosed since the 16th century. The hedges on this walk are also typical of our old English countryside with trees sticking up at intervals to provide shade and shelter for cattle.

Head towards Beeston Castle as you cross the next field and come to a stile to the right of a stagnant pond. Negotiate this and a ditch, then keep along the right-hand side of the field until you reach a stile under an ash tree, which takes you onto Pudding Lane.

4. Turn right and immediately left through a steel kissing gate, joining the Sandstone Trail as it continues towards Beeston Castle. Keep ahead along a hedge, passing a tennis court before crossing a sturdily-built bridge into the next field, where the way is ahead again. Keep forward after another kissing gate, walking down the side of the field until you bear right in the corner to exit via another kissing gate. Cross the road here and walk straight across the facing field which rolls down to Wharton's Lock, where you leave the Sandstone Trail.

The waterway here is the Shropshire Union canal, built in 1775 to link the Midlands to Chester. Also notice the milestone signifying that this is almost the halfway point of the Sandstone Trail. Beeston Castle, perched precariously high on its hill, looks as if it could topple off at any moment. The River Gowy and the railway run parallel to the canal here and this is a delightful picnic spot.

A curved bridge over the Shropshire Union Canal at Wharton's Lock, leads the eye to distant Beeston Crag

5. Walk across the footbridge and turn right along the towpath under stone bridge No. 108.

Look for the rope marks still clearly visible on the bridge's sides. Also notice the brick and concrete shelter for the stop planks – a typical canal feature.

Leave the canal at Bates Mill Bridge, passing the original mill, now a private house, and crossing the bridge. Continue up the road past the Shady Oak pub and, on reaching Huxley Lane, keep ahead through a steel kissing gate.

6. Cross the field bearing right until you reach a stile in the facing hedge, just to the right of a gap in the hedge. Keep to the right again over the next field to stiles and a plank bridge in the far corner. In the third field veer right, passing a marshy pond on your left to a stile under an wizened oak.

Cross the fourth field, following the fence on your right all the way to its end. Go over a stile and pass a pond on your left. Continue in the same direction to a plank bridge and a stile where you join the Sandstone Trail again. Keep ahead on a clear path across four fields until you reach a signpost and turn right towards Tarporley, leaving the Sandstone Trail.

7. Leave the field via a steel gate. Walk around the perimeter of the next very long field, crossing a wooden stile halfway along. Turn left at the far end through a metal kissing gate. Then, after 20 metres, go right through a steel gate.

8. From here walk ahead up the right-hand side of the dry valley and mewing buzzards may accompany you to the bypass. Cross with caution. Follow the fence ahead, then drop down to a stile and a track. Cross this and keep ahead down the right-hand side of two fields, then continue into a free public car park behind the Rising Sun – an alternative start for the walk perhaps. Continue through this and turn right down Tarporley High Street back to your car.

Tarporley

A brass band passes Tarporley's elegant Georgian Swan Hotel during the annual Tarporley Carnival

Walking down the High Street, straightaway you pass the Rising Sun, a very old pub with a Preservation Order on it. Notice too the milestone tucked against the wall here. You're only 172 miles from London.

And it would be hard to miss the imposing Swan Hotel. Built in 1769, it became an important coaching inn on the route from London and the Midlands to Chester and Holyhead.

Also look for the 'listed' telephone box adjacent to the post office – one of the few remaining traditional kiosks designed by Sir Giles Gilbert Scott in 1935.

15. Davenham

Delightful views, then a peaceful stroll beside a canal and back along country lanes

River Dane, Shipbrook Hill, Gad Brook, Trent & Mersey Canal, Manor Lane, Shipbrook Bridge

Start: *Lay-by near the River Dane. Map reference: SJ 671711.*

By Car: *Take the A533 south from Northwich. Keep straight on to Davenham at the Northwich by-pass (A556) roundabout. In the village turn left down Church Street, passing the church and driving over the A533. Park in the lay-by on the right before crossing the River Dane.*

Distance: *4 miles/6.5 kilometres.*

Duration: *Allow 2 hours.*

Difficulty: *Easy.*

Food and Drink: *Bull's Head (01606 43725) and Oddfellows Arms (01606 227809) in Davenham. Riverside Organics (01606 46258) is within sight at the walk's end.*

Map: *OS 1:25,000 Explorer 267 Northwich & Delamere Forest.*

The walk

1. Walk ahead, crossing the River Dane (a tributary of the River Mersey) on Shipbrook Bridge – an elegant sandstone structure.

The River Dane rises on Axe Edge in the Peak District, then meanders across the Cheshire Plain, skirting Congleton and Middlewich before joining the Weaver Navigation in Northwich.

The first part of this walk provides delightful views as you breast Shipbrook Hill, and the piercing spire, 99 feet/30 metres high, of Davenham's Victorian church, is a distinctive landmark along much of the route.

Davenham

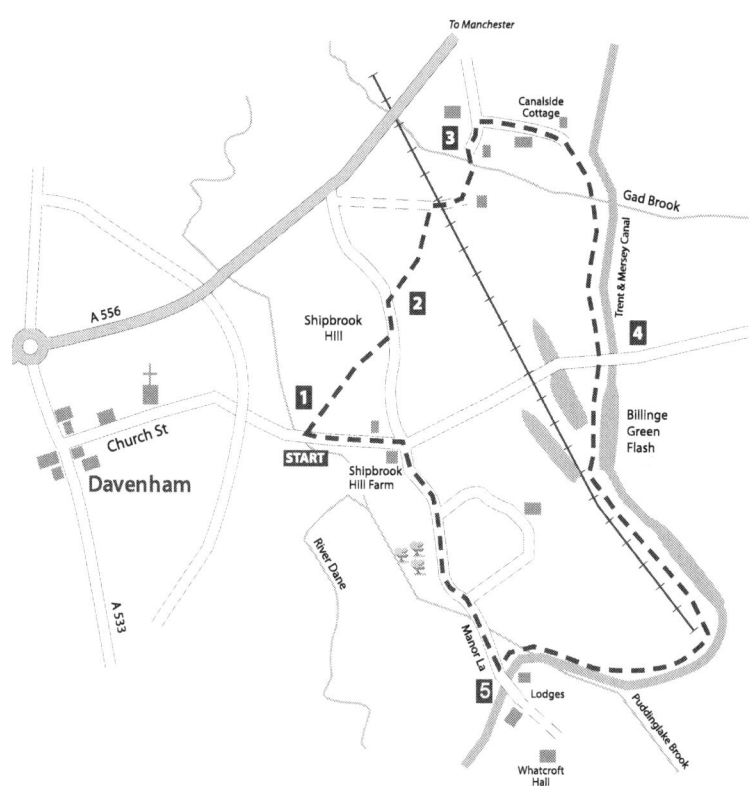

Immediately, turn left over a stile and make for the corner of the hedge, walking down this, which can be wet, to a lonely stile to the left of a magnificent oak. From here, climb straight up the hill in the same direction, to a stile in the hedge at the top. Then follow the path across the next field to another stile and turn left along the country lane for a very short distance.

2. Turn right when you reach two metal gates on your right and walk down the field with the hedge on your right. The railway bridge eventually comes into view ahead and, at the end of the field, turn right onto the farm road and cross the railway. Straightaway, turn left over a stile, dropping down to cross a rough field diagonally right until the path crosses Gad Brook.

(As I understand it, this is a permissive path to avoid walkers having to pass between all the buildings around Park Farm then wend their way back to Gad Bridge through even worse nettles.)

3. Cross the brook and continue over a stile and up a footpath which becomes a rough road. You then pass between business premises, with Gadbrook Business Centre on your right. Keep ahead until you reach a high wooden fence on your left and, where the lane starts to rise, bear right down a path to the Trent & Mersey Canal. Turn right along the towpath, away from bridge 182 and passing what used to be Orchard Marina.

This once busy waterway was built to join the industrial Midlands to the port of Liverpool. Today, this peaceful pathway passes pleasure craft and fishermen. You might even disturb a heron fishing, and, with luck, the sun may be shimmering on the water.

The rusting carcass of a narrowboat decorates the broad salt subsidence lake at Billinge Flash, near Davenham

You soon walk under the Brine Pipe Bridge. Built in 1935 to carry brine from Holford, on the Plumley walk, to the salt works at Winsford and Middlewich, it now carries water from the River Dane to Lostock, near Northwich.

4. Pass Park Farm Marina on your right, then continue under bridge 181.

Several features of the canal can be seen along here, including the unusual iron milestones and stop-planks under a corrugated iron roof. Beyond bridge 181, on the left Oakwood Marina is home to many boats and a cafe. To reach it cross the bridge then return the same way.

Billinge Green Flash is one of several areas where the original bank has disappeared completely and large areas of lake have formed, probably caused by salt extraction. These places have become reed-fringed meres – a water birds' paradise.

For some distance, the railway runs parallel with the canal before you cross a causeway and walk under the iron bridge, supported by brick pillars, which takes it away. As you walk on, a country road runs alongside and you pass the derelict remains of a bridge festooned with ivy. Tall grasses, wild rose, cow parsley, pink campion and speedwell brighten the banks until, eventually, Puddinglake Brook, a tributary of the River Dane, flows deep down under the canal below a coppice of mixed woodland. At the end of this are several giant beech trees with silvery grey boles and wide canopies which spread out across the water.

5. Eventually you reach bridge 179 and the black-and-white facades of the original lodges to Whatcroft Hall. Leave the canal here, climbing sandstone steps and turning right along Manor Lane. Ignore two right turns, between which you cross the stream again as it ripples through a bluebell wood. You then pass Shipbrook Hill Farm where Riverside Organics is a thriving business, selling refreshments and commanding a splendid view. Finally, when you reach a crossroads, turn left towards Davenham, crossing Shipbrook Bridge at the walk's end.

16. Great Budworth

Meres, flashes, a canal and a boat lift – one of the great wonders of Cheshire

Budworth Mere, Kennel Wood, Cogshall Lane, Anderton Boat Lift, Trent & Mersey Canal, Marston, Great Budworth

Start: *Lay-by on Budworth Lane. Map reference: SJ 656774.*

By Car: *Take the A559 north from Northwich. After passing through Higher Marston and rounding a wide bend take the next left turn up Budworth Lane. A small parking area can be found on the right where the road is straight and wide.*

Distance: *6.5 miles/10.5 kilometres.*

Duration: *Allow 3 to 4 hours.*

Difficulty: *Easy-medium. One or two slight inclines.*

Food and Drink: *Anderton Boat Lift (01606 872868); Anderton Marina (01606 79642); Stanley Arms (01606 75059) in Anderton; The Salt Barge in Marston (01606 43064), The George & Dragon (01606 891317) in Great Budworth.*

Map: *OS 1:25,000 Explorer 267 Northwich & Delamere Forest.*

The walk

1. Walk ahead past Brownslow House and Brownslow Cottage before turning left into the wood at the footpath sign. Drop down between towering sycamores and emerge to cross the field ahead where Budworth Mere comes into view.

It was used as a fish hatchery in the Middle Ages and even now is well stocked with bream and pike. Reed warblers and great crested grebe breed in its reeds. Marbury Country Park borders its southern shore and is well worth a visit.

You eventually join the fence on your right, keeping alongside it to avoid the lower ground which tends to be boggy. Continue

Great Budworth

forward through a kissing gate and over a stream, which has a wide bridge for cows and farm vehicles, and a sturdy footbridge with handrails for walkers. Keep ahead, with the barbed wire fence on your right, to a sturdy kissing gate, then cross parkland to go through another kissing gate in the hedge, to reach the road.

2. Turn left, then right through a kissing gate and down a footpath to Anderton. With the hawthorn hedge on your right, walk forward, then another kissing gate takes you into Kennel Wood. Cross a sturdy bridge over Cogshall Brook, the clear water burbling over its sandy bed, and, in late spring, the area is awash with pink campion, ramsons, bluebells and wood anemones.

After climbing over a stile out of the wood, keep forward across the field to the stile at the side of the gate ahead. Claycroft Farm is to your right and the path up the next field is very clearly defined. As you negotiate a stile and turn left along Cogshall Lane an industrial landscape comes into view.

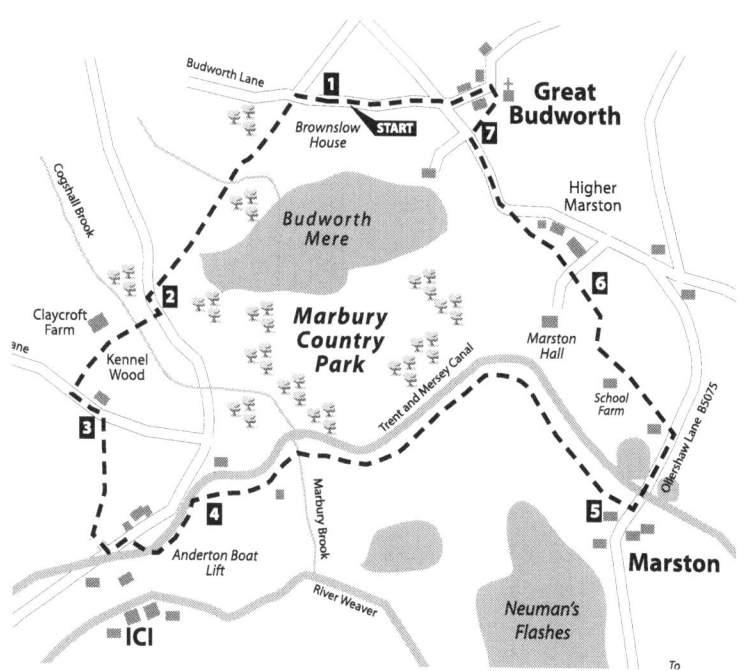

Although in decline, the vastness of ICI's Mond Division works at Winnington still fills the skyline and it is easy to see how Northwich was once known as 'The Black Country of the North'.

3. When you reach a house on your left, turn right onto a footpath. Cross the field to the wide gap in the opposite hedge, then keep ahead with the field boundary on your right. After the next stile veer slightly left to a further stile by a gate in the facing fence. After two more stiles the final one is across a small field, by a huge hawthorn bush in the hedge's left-hand corner.

Another stile takes you to a track that you follow before turning left along the road into Anderton. Then take the next right turn down Old Road to the Anderton Boat Lift, passing Holmeswood, a coach firm and the Stanley Arms.

The Anderton Boat Lift is one of the wonders of Cheshire. This incredible construction was the first of its kind in the world and is the only one now in use in Britain. It raises and lowers boats 50 feet/15 metres between the Trent & Mersey Canal and the River Weaver.

Using a system of locks, this used to take well over an hour but the lift reduced the time to five minutes. It was first opened in 1875, and its hydraulic mechanism was converted to an electric operation in 1907.

The lift was closed by the British Water Board in August 1983 as the main support legs were badly corroded. After many protests about its prolonged closure it was finally re-opened in 2002 and is now one of Cheshire's most important attractions.

Cross the footbridge over the canal and turn left, passing the main entrance to the Visitor Centre, cafe and gift shop. Then continue along the towpath. The Anderton Nature Park provides a sheltered picnic spot, and both working barges and pleasure craft line the banks.

4. Common reeds wave in the wind as you walk under rectangular bridges and past old iron signposts indicating the mileage between Preston Brook and Shardlow – the canal's length. You soon reach Anderton Marina with its fleet of brightly-coloured narrow boats for hire, plus a gift shop and pleasant cafe.

Now celebrated as the 'Cathedral of the Canals', the Anderton Lift carries narrowboats between the Trent & Mersey Canal and the Weaver Navigation

Cross the bridge which goes over the cut to the Upland Basin Marina, and continue along the towpath. On opposite banks, Hopyards and Uplands are woodlands newly created as part of the Mersey Forest. Beside a cottage called Jackson's Turn, a run-off drops steeply down to Marbury Brook.

Along here the canal forms the southern boundary of Marbury Country Park – a large country estate from the 13th century until the 1930s. You may get a glimpse of parkland through the trees of Big Wood – gloriously carpeted by bluebells in late spring – and an elegant black-and-white footbridge will take you into it if you wish to explore further.

Leaving the woodland behind, ahead is the village of Marston. You pass another black-and-white iron signpost and may already have noticed sturdy iron rings set in concrete, for mooring boats. This stretch of the canal is to stride along, especially in a nippy wind. A brightly-coloured sign advertises the Salt Barge – an apt name for the popular pub here. Leave the towpath at the bridge.

The area still accounts for two-thirds of the rock salt produced in this country for use on roads in winter and in front of you stands the Lion Salt Works. The only place still producing salt by the 'open pan' method until it went bankrupt in 1986, it serves as a reminder that the prosperity of Northwich has been based on salt since Roman times. Now preserved as a heritage centre it is open to the public on certain days.

Over to your right Neuman's Flash is the largest of the salt lakes. Known as 'flashes' these meres are the result of the subsidence of old salt workings.

You can glimpse Witton church from here. The oldest building in Northwich, its roof came from Norton Priory, near Runcorn, and its tower was built by Thomas Hunter, who also constructed the tower of Great Budworth church.

5. Turn left onto Ollershaw Lane (B5075) perhaps pausing on the bridge to look back at Marston village.

This was built on pillars of salt that are slowly dissolving. Many foundations have now been stabilised but in the past whole houses were lost, tumbling without warning into old brine pits, and others lining the switchback street used to look as if they were about to topple.

Continue along the road between two smaller flashes.

These were also the result of subsidence caused by the pumping out of brine from beneath the surface. Bullrushes, reeds and flag iris fringe the banks and these wild areas are the haunt of swans, ducks, coots and anglers.

Ahead is Marston's church hall, built in 1908 adjacent to the ancient graveyard. Sadly, the church was demolished many years ago.

Immediately after passing a furniture business turn left along tarmac, then a rough track. Keep to the right of the gate to School Farm, walking ahead at the field's edge to a metal kissing gate. Keep forward, with the fence now on your right, to another kissing gate. Then cross the next field diagonally, heading towards Great Budworth church.

6. After another kissing gate walk alongside the fence to cross the track to Marston Hall, before continuing behind houses to another kissing gate. Walk down the side of this final field to a corner kissing gate, which takes you onto the A559. Cross to the safety of the opposite footpath and turn left.

On your left is Budworth Mere, used by the local sailing club, where the members' boats, their tall masts leaning at haphazard angles, cluster around the clubhouse.

The crenellated tower of Great Budworth church has been a prominent landmark on much of this walk and is visible in great detail here. Constructed of large blocks of local sandstone, the building dates from the 14th century and is one of the great parish churches of Cheshire, at one time servicing the largest parish in the county, which consisted of 35 townships. In the south aisle chapel are five 13th century oak stalls – probably the oldest examples of such furniture in the county – and there is also a fine 15th century font.

7. To explore Great Budworth village, a rare bit of Tudor England, and perhaps visit the George and Dragon, turn right off the road

Great Budworth is arguably Cheshire's loveliest village

and walk diagonally up the field on a clear pathway. Turn right along the hedge at the top and continue through a metal gate and along a wide grass path between hedges. Veer left at the end over a tarmac driveway, turning left again behind the church.

The church is the centrepiece of this pretty picture-book village and has been described as, 'a church sitting on a knoll with cottages clustered around it like a hen with her chicks'. The village was much restored and rebuilt in the 19th century by Rowland Egerton-Warburton of Arley Hall as Great Budworth was then still part of the Arley estate.

Notice the stocks near the lychgate, and the old schoolhouse standing in the churchyard. Built in Shakespeare's time, stone foundations support its brick walls and gabled roof, and tiny mullioned windows let in some light. The oldest houses stand opposite this, on School Lane.

Once a coaching inn, the George and Dragon dates from 1722, its studded oak door topped by a massive stone lintel two feet thick. Above the door is one of the rhymes composed by Egerton Warburton ...

>As Saint George in armed array
>Did the fiery dragon slay;
>So mayst thou with might no less
>Slay the dragon drunkenness.

As you pass the stocks and turn left down the High Street notice the huge Elizabethan chimneys and the names and dates on the cottages. Bakery Cottage must once have been the local bakery. Revel in this delightful English village as you drop down the hill to the ancient pumphouse.

The villagers only source of drinking water until 1934, the pumphouse features a rhyme that thanks God for the underground spring that surfaces here. Pause to admire the ornate iron door of this ancient wooden structure.

Then cross the A559 with care and walk up Budworth Lane back to your car.

17. Little Budworth

Magical woodland, soft sandy soil and the dappled shade of silver birch

Budworth Pool, Coach Road, Little Budworth Common, Oulton Mill, Dogmore Lane, Moss Hall Farm, outskirts of Oulton Park, Little Budworth

> **Start:** *The east end of Budworth Pool. Map reference: SJ 600656.*
>
> **By Car:** *Take the A49 south from Warrington. After the A54 traffic lights, take the next left turn (down the Coach Road) to Little Budworth. Turn left when you reach the gates of Oulton Park motor racing circuit. Drive through the village and keep left round the bend after the church, dropping downhill. Budworth Pool is then on the left. Park there or continue uphill and park on the left.*
>
> **Distance:** *5.5 miles/9 kilometres.*
>
> **Duration:** *Allow 3 hours.*
>
> **Difficulty:** *Easy.*
>
> **Food and Drink:** *Red Lion (01829 760275) in Little Budworth.*
>
> **Map:** *OS 1:25,000 Explorer 267 Northwich & Delamere Forest.*

The walk

1. Return downhill and turn right over a stile which takes you alongside this pretty reed-fringed fishing pool. About halfway along its length (at the end of a fence) turn right again over a stile. Cross the field, climbing over two more stiles, then turn left along a path which sinks between banks topped by bramble, blackthorn, hawthorn and bracken – a typical feature of the Cheshire countryside. A cart-track, edged with a profusion of wildflowers, then takes you to Park Road.

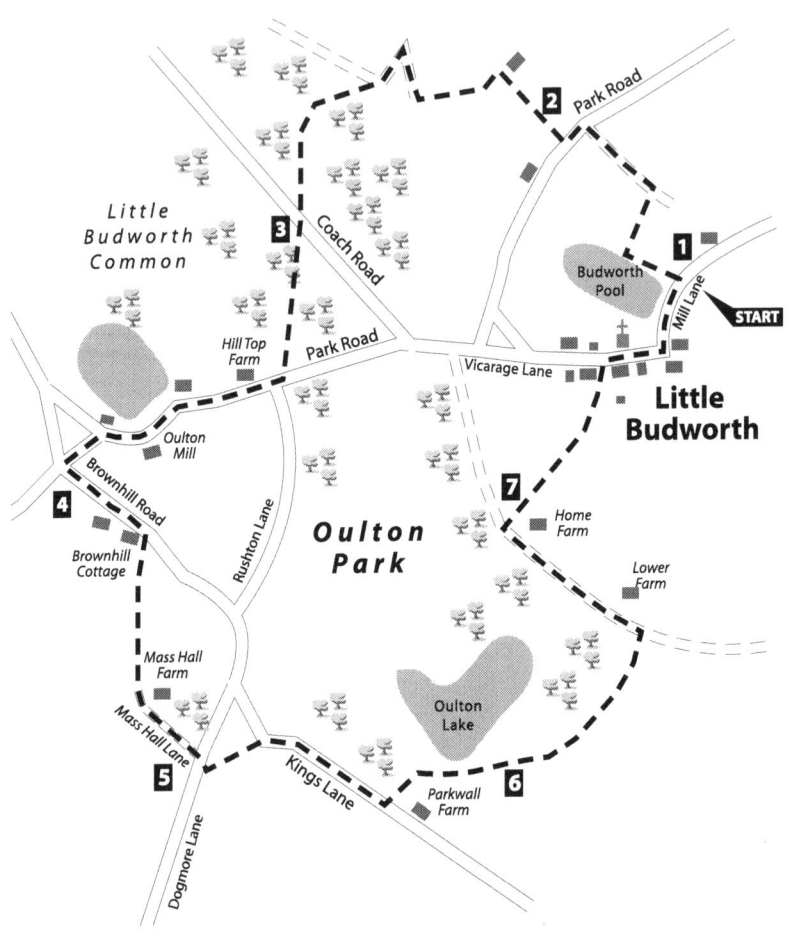

2. Turn left and immediately right over a stile signposted to Whitehall Lane. (Yellow arrows at each stile indicate clearly which way to go.) Walk across the field to a stile just to the left of the house ahead. Turn left to another stile, then cross the field diagonally, skirting the wood until you come to a stile into it in the far corner. Then turn right along the fence to a final stile.

Go straight ahead at this sandy junction, following the clear stream to another junction, where you turn left over it.

Watercress was once produced commercially for the London markets in the clear, sandy-bedded streams here. And while crossing this one I was lucky enough to see a kingfisher arrow straight up the wide stream, its metallic blue and orange colouring shimmering in the sun.

The track winds uphill past one or two houses, then continues as a broad dirt road. Ignore all paths off it and you will soon reach the Coach Road at a triangle of Scots pine.

This road was built in the 18th century as a long, straight drive up to the gates of Oulton Park, which was then a large estate owned by the Egerton family. Oulton Hall was later destroyed by fire but the grand ornamental gates, designed by Vanburgh, still stand.

3. Cross the road to enter a lovely stretch of common.

The sandy soil has never been worth cultivating and this woodland, where silver birches predominate, has an almost ethereal quality.

Walk on this soft sandy ride to Park Road. Turn right here, passing Hill Top Farm.

Oulton Mill—before the fire which destroyed the business.

Oulton Mill Pool is an attractive spot and Oulton Mill (alongside the road) was a corn mill before being converted into a craft centre, selling antiques and reproduction furniture until a fire gutted it.

4. Continue uphill, then at the crossroads turn left onto Brownhill Road. After passing thatched Brownhill Cottage, a little gem built in 1675, turn right over a stile by a steel gate. Cross the field diagonally left to a stile about halfway along the hedge, then cross the next field diagonally right to another stile. Walk up the final field making for the outbuildings of Moss Hall Farm, where you head for three metal silos, then make your way to a squat round silo. Continue through the yard, past the farmhouse and down Moss Hall Lane.

5. At Dogmore Lane, a Victorian postbox is set into the wall opposite as you turn right and immediately left through a gate. Cross two fields to reach Kings Lane and turn right. Then, just before Parkwall Farm, turn left over a stile. Walk down to the wall at the bottom of the field and turn right over another stile.

This tall brick wall is a relic from the Oulton Park estate and you may glimpse Oulton Lake and the motor racing circuit through gaps in it. Oulton Park is a premier venue for motor racing in England.

6. Continue beside the wall, crossing five more stiles, the final one at the end of the hedge after the wall ends. After this, don't go over the stile on the right but walk down the field with the hedge on your right. At the far end exit over a stile, cross a stream, turn left along a lane and you soon pass the Lower Farm of the Darley Hall estate.

Little Budworth church tower and the houses of the village come into view as you continue along here, passing Home Farm with its neat buildings grouped in a rectangle round an open, now only partly-cobbled, yard – a good example of the way dairy farms were built in the 19th century.

7. After this climb over a stile on the right beside the second oak. Drop straight down the field to a dry valley – once having a stream full of bright green, healthy watercress. Cross the three stones across the mush and climb uphill, making for a stile between two gates. Then keep the hedge on your left as you walk along the side of two more fields. Continue forward down Booth Avenue and turn right onto Vicarage Lane.

You may wish to picnic on the attractive village green along here and it is worth pausing to look at the church. The oldest part is the tower. Ornamented by numerous faces and gargoyles it is thought to be of secular origin. The bright, spacious interior boasts the widest unsupported church roof in Cheshire and, behind the organ, the plough window celebrates the Millennium. In 1745 Henry Lovett, King of the Gypsies, was buried in the graveyard.

The Red Lion has had a licence since 1797 and, with a blazing fire in winter and homemade food, this traditional village inn makes everyone feel at home.

At the far end of the churchyard turn left into Mill Lane and drop down the slope back to your car.

Little Budworth church seen across the reed-fringed Budworth Pool

18. Little Leigh

A canal, a tunnel, fields and woodland

Little Leigh, Trent & Mersey Canal, Saltersford Tunnel, Barnton, Stone Heyes Lane, Deslay Heath Farm, Clatterwick Lane

> **Start:** *Near Clatterwick Lane. Map reference: SJ 618772.*
>
> **By Car:** *Take the A49 from Warrington. Turn left at Dones Green onto the A533 to Barnton and Northwich. Take the first left turn and, after passing Ash Tree Farm, park beside the road just before Clatterwick Lane.*
>
> **Distance:** *5 miles/8 kilometres.*
>
> **Duration:** *Allow 2 to 3 hours.*
>
> **Difficulty:** *Easy. Muddy in places.*
>
> **Food and Drink:** *A Spar shop at the petrol station in Barnton sells snacks.*
>
> **Map:** *OS 1:25,000 Explorer 267 Northwich & Delamere Forest.*

The walk

1. Walk forward and turn right onto a footpath that starts off down the drive of house number 39. Cross the field with the hedge on your right and continue to another stile, then drop down the next field to a stream. Walk straight up the following field, making for a visible stile on the horizon in a hedge corner. Keep the hedge on your right as you continue down the final field to another stile and the A533.

2. Cross this busy road with care. Turn left then immediately right down a footpath with a hawthorn hedge on your right and the slim spire of St Michael's church in Little Leigh ahead. Carry on up the next field to the stile, which takes you into yet another field. Keep the fence on your right, negotiate another stile and continue in the same direction (the hedge now on your left) to Leigh Lane.

3. Turn right along this country lane for a short distance before turning left down a cart-track, which winds between mixed hedgerows – so typical of Cheshire. The main track ends at a field but you keep forward towards a small wood, enjoying far-reaching views. Follow the little stream gurgling busily down through its wooded valley, carpeted by wood anemones, then bluebells, in early summer. The path may be muddy so take care.

Turn left along another country lane, bordered by celandines in spring, cross a bridge and drop down through a gap in the fence to the Trent & Mersey Canal. Then turn right along the towpath towards Barnton.

Over your right shoulder you can soon spot the swing bridge which spans the River Weaver at Acton Bridge. Along here the canal hugs a ledge above the Weaver's wide valley and the two waterways run very close together, in places only a field's width apart.

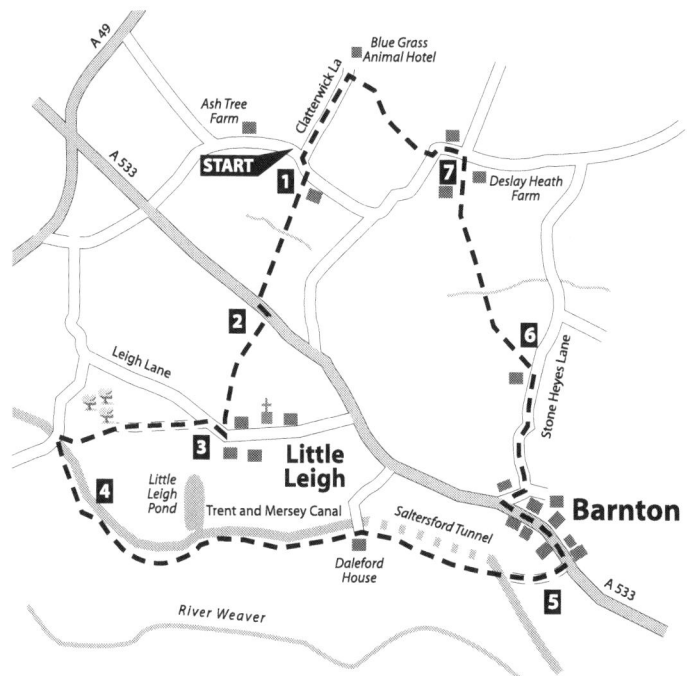

Brightly-coloured boats lie moored along the canal bank, stands of common reeds waft gently in the breeze and the sturdy bulk of St Mary's church in Weaverham can be seen above this ever-expanding village.

Look out for the unusual cast iron, two-armed mileposts too. Unique to this canal, they give the distances from each end, in this instance Shardlow 88 miles and Preston Brook 4 miles.

4. You eventually pass under the arch of a pretty, white-painted bridge in the middle of absolutely nowhere.

Look out for Little Leigh pond on the opposite bank, a delightful unspoilt spot teeming with wildlife. Ramsons (wild garlic) edge the towpath in spring as you approach bridge No. 204 and Daleford House.

Then continue along the towpath to Saltersford Tunnel.

One of the earliest canal tunnels, it will only take one narrow boat at a time and, in the early days, boatmen would have to leg it through as there is no towpath for a horse. The old wooden posts where boats would tie up to await their turn are also still visible.

Passing a white-painted house, walk up the old horsepath and along the top of the tunnel.

Notice another canal signpost here. On its base, R and D are the initials of the firm which erected it and the date was 1819. Look out for the short brick tower in the adjacent field – an air-vent for the tunnel below – before you drop down to the canal again. Saltersford Tunnel was repaired and re-opened to canal traffic in 1984. It bends slightly, so one end is not visible from the other.

5. Leave the towpath here, veering left uphill, then along Leigh's Brow into Barnton where you turn left. Notice the George VI postbox in the wall along here before passing a petrol station and Spar shop. Then turn right up Stone Heyes Lane and sharp left to walk out of the village.

6. Turn left down a footpath just past Stone Heyes Farm, where periwinkle's mauve star-shaped flowers peep from the hedgerow. Pass a duckpond, then veer diagonally across this field, making for the pylon in the far corner where a sturdy bridge is hidden. With the hedge on your right walk down the next field to a steel

A narrowboat emerging from the Barnton end of the Saltersford Tunnel, on the Trent & Mersey Canal

gate. Then continue forward down the track to pass Desley Heath Farm.

7. Turn left at the road, signposted to Dones Green and Little Leigh. After a sharp bend turn right through a steel kissing gate, then cross the field diagonally, making for the top right-hand corner. Go through a kissing gate here and walk forward, below the brow of the hill to a track. Turn left along this, cross the bridge over the stream and, at Blue Grass Animal Hotel, turn left and walk down Clatterwick Lane back to your car.

19. Lower Whitley

Wildflowers abound on this country stroll

Whitley Hall, Merryfall Wood, Back Lane, Village Lane

Start: *Opposite the Chetwode Arms in the village.*
Map reference: SJ 615789.

By Car: *Take the A49 south from Warrington. Take the first left turn into Lower Whitley and park at the top end of the village where the road is wide.*

Distance: *3 miles/5 kilometres.*

Duration: *Allow 1 to 2 hours.*

Difficulty: *Easy.*

Food and Drink: *Chetwode Arms (01925 730203)*

Map: *OS 1:25,000 Explorer 267 Northwich & Delamere Forest.*

The walk

1. Walk down the village street to The Chetwode Arms which used to be the meeting place for the hunt.

You may spot the old AA sign on the end of the converted barns opposite. The faded words state that you are 177½ miles from London.

The footpath you want leads off to the left opposite the inn's entrance. The path then skirts the churchyard.

The church itself dates from the 17th century and has a glorious Jacobean hammerbeam roof. Curiously, the timber lychgate – a memorial to men who died in the 1st World War – houses the church clock.

Climb over the stile at the end of this path and keep to the right as you cross the small meadow to a stile in the corner. Cross the next field to the visible stile, bear left beside the hedge to a gate and turn right along the track to Whitley Hall.

2. Just before the farmhouse turn left over a stile and walk round two sides of the garden then on to a corner stile. From here make for a reed-fringed pool teeming with wildlife, passing it on your left. You will then see a stile in the hedge on your left.

Walk down the next field with the fence on your right. Climb over the stile in this, then stay in the same direction to enter Merryfall Wood. Keep ahead through this until you turn left over a stile (or go through a gap in the hedge just before this) then continue with the wood on your right.

Notice the abundance of wild flowers, bluebells and pink campion in late spring, and others later on.

3. At the wood's end keep ahead along the track to Merryfall, where you bear left along a rough road. Ignore the immediate left turn then bear left at a T-junction to Lester House Farm.

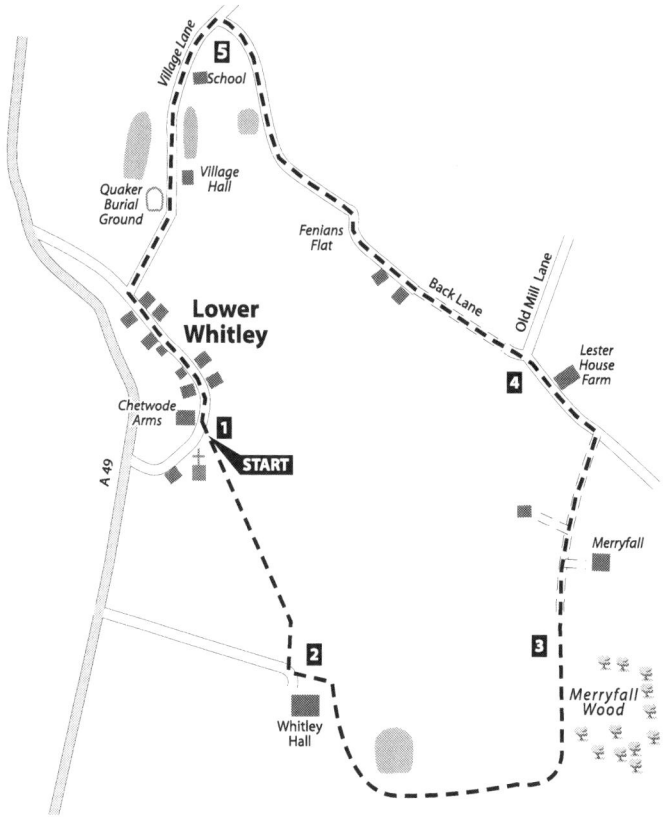

This curious timber lychgate at Lower Whitley contains the church clock.

4. When Old Mill Lane branches right keep ahead along Back Lane which, for some distance, becomes a very rough track, then a footpath to a tarmac road.

On the left here you pass a much extended dwelling, now called Poacher's Lodge but originally known as Fenian's Cottage. Behind it is a flat piece of land hemmed in and sheltered by banks on all sides. Long ago cattle were driven from Ireland to Liverpool and this area made a convenient overnight stop. Fenian was the name of the drover who used this route and the land became known as Fenian's Flat.

5. At the lane's end turn left along Village Lane back to your car.

The attractive primary school dates from 1875 and beyond it fishing pools lie on either side of the road. Many of these have been formed as a result of the extensive sand quarrying in this area.

Opposite the village hall is a sandstone wall, behind which lies Frandley's Quaker Burial Ground. This peaceful spot dates back to 1657, a time when Quakers could not to be buried in consecrated ground.

20. Plumley

A magical path through Holford Moss, industrial relics and a wonderful ancient hall

Trouthall Lane, Peover Eye, Holford Moss, Langford Farm, Holford Hall

Start: *Trouthall Lane, Plumley. Map reference: SJ 717753.*

By Car: *Take the A556 from Northwich, driving east towards Manchester. Turn right to Plumley at The Smoker, an inn since Elizabethan times, named after a famous racehorse.*

Drive through Plumley village. There is limited parking at the entrance to the station on the left or, over the railway bridge, at the Golden Pheasant pub on the right, with permission.

Distance: *4 miles/6.5 kilometres.*

Duration: *Allow 2 hours.*

Difficulty: *Easy. Muddy in places. This walk is probably best negotiated early or late in the year before bracken obliterates the path through Holford Moss.*

Food and Drink: *The Smoker (01565 722338); Golden Pheasant (01565 722261) which serves food until 2.30pm in the week and all day at weekends.*

Map: *OS 1:25,000 Explorer 267 Northwich & Delamere Forest.*

The walk

1. Opposite the entrance to the station car park, go down rough South Drive. At the end of this continue down a snicket, then turn right, and right again, along Yew Tree Road. At its end turn left down Trouthall Lane. Where this bends left keep ahead down a narrow 'No Through Road'. Cross over a broad stream named the Peover Eye and turn immediately right over a stile.

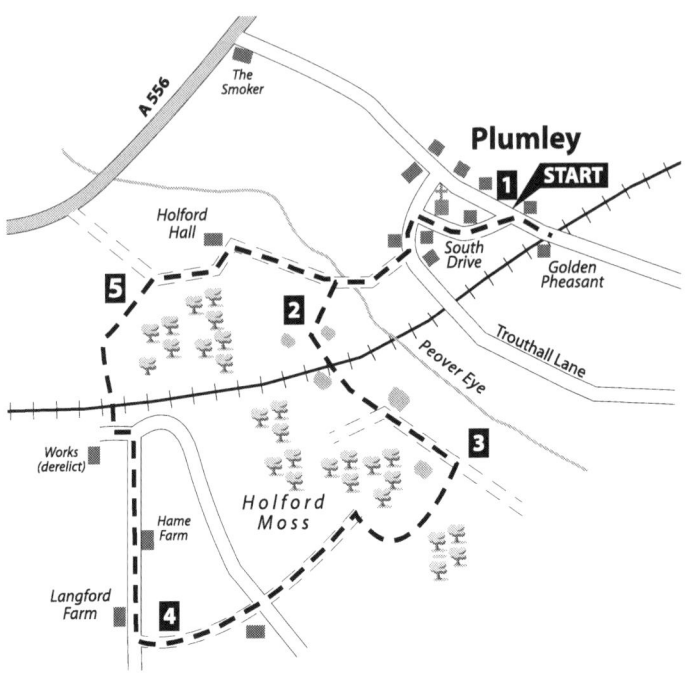

Continue ahead along a farm track between hedgerows. At the end of the first field, where this veers right, turn left along the side of the field

2. Pass a tree-fringed pond, then bear left before another, after which the path goes ahead across the field and up over the railway line, which connects Manchester and Chester, on a brick bridge. Continue forward and along the side of a field, then go straight on at the next field along the track to a cattle grid on a farm road. Turn left along this, passing more ponds, to a stile beside a gate.

3. Go through the gate and continue past wholly rebuilt Keeper's Lodge. *The adjacent area here was once a pheasant reserve on the Holford estate.* Immediately past the house turn right into a wood known as Holford Moss. Keep to the right, following the fence along the edge of the wood at first.

At one time large areas of lowland Cheshire were covered by peaty tracts of land, much of which was gradually reclaimed. Mosses, moors or heaths, often along river valleys covered with peat, were frequently used as common pasture and were places where people would dig turves for their fires before coal became cheap.

On this part of the walk you can feel the soft peaty texture of the soil underfoot as you meander along on this brambly, bracken-fringed path through thin woodland, where holly and silver birch predominate. *This is a magical part of the walk especially when sunlight filters through the branches.*

You eventually drop down a slope and bear left to cross a stream on a narrow wooden footbridge. Leaving the wood

Derelict pipes and wellheads marooned in the fields around Plumley are reminders of Cheshire's ancient brine-pumping industry

behind, walk up the side of two rough fields, then along a track to the road, which you follow all the way to Langford Farm.

The remains of derricks and rusty pipes littering the roadside and fields are the detritus of the brine pumping industry which used to take place here, and latterly storage was in huge cavities, deep underground.

4. Turn right at the farm and you soon pass Hame Farm. Then continue through scrubby woodland to a T-junction and the railway line.

On your left you have just passed the overgrown remains of the Octel Works. Opened in 1939, it produced aircraft fuel during the 2nd World War and was known as the Jam Plant to divert suspicion. It closed in 1986.

A signal box may be visible away to your right but you turn left, then almost immediately right, through a narrow gate in the metal security fence. Cross the railway line with extreme caution and continue forward.

Hidden in the overgrown woodland on your right here are derelict buildings where munitions were made during the 1st World War.

At a crossing of tracks keep straight ahead.

Up to your right are the overgrown Plumley Lime Beds. Formed by lime slurry waste from a nearby chemical works, these extend over 58 acres/24 hectares. Still owned by ICI, they are now managed by the Cheshire Wildlife Trust as a nature reserve and Site of Special Scientific Interest, where ten species of sedge and several types of orchid can be found. The area also provides nesting sites for blackcap, garden and willow warblers, and lesser whitethroat, while the lagoon attracts waders and ducks, including common sandpipers, greenshanks and teal.

5. Holford Hall eventually comes into view.

Gloriously half-timbered, the present hall was built around 1620 near the site of a previous hall thought to have dated from the 13th century. It was built for Mary Cholmondeley, the last heiress and survivor of the Holford family. The building was originally three-sided and the oak timbers of its frame were blackened by pitch or tar to contrast with the white-washed wattle-and-daub, or brick, infilling.

Though still noteworthy today, much of Elizabethan Holford Hall was demolished in the 1880s

There was also a gatehouse and drawbridge and, in its heyday, the hall employed up to 60 people, including dairy maids, cheese maids, governesses, farmhands and seamstresses. However, by 1884 only the main building survived and a century later it was in a rather sorry state. However today, set in beautiful grounds, it looks superb.

Continue on the track, following the field's edge until you join up with the early part of the walk and return to your car.

21. Acton Bridge

A waterway walk through pleasant countryside

Acton Brook, Acton Bridge, River Weaver, Dutton Locks, Cliff Lane, Crowton

> **Start:** *Crowton. Map reference: SJ 579745.*
>
> **By Car:** *Take the A49 from Warrington. Turn right immediately after crossing the River Weaver. At Acton Bridge station turn right to Crowton. As you enter the village there is room for one car to park on the right, just before the 30mph sign. However, the owner of the Hare and Hounds pub, on the left, has given permission for cars to be parked in his car park. (Out of politeness please contact him if several cars are involved.)*
>
> **Distance:** *5 miles/8 kilometres.*
>
> **Duration:** *Allow 3 hours.*
>
> **Difficulty:** *Easy. Muddy in places.*
>
> **Food and Drink:** *Hare & Hounds (01928 788851) in Crowton; Leigh Arms, by the swing bridge on the A49, which serves food all day. (01606 853327)*
>
> **Maps:** *OS 1:25,000 Explorer 267 Northwich & Delamere Forest.*

The walk

1. Walk back along the road towards Acton Bridge and, after passing Grange Cottage, turn left down a grassy lane. The mass of Frodsham Hill is clearly visible as you walk along between two neatly clipped hawthorn hedges, frothing with cow parsley in early summer. You soon come to the attractive Acton Mill complex where Acton Brook has been artificially widened to make a large pleasant pool and the water overflows noisily on its way down to the River Weaver.

2. Continue ahead, negotiating two stiles, then keep down the left-hand side of the field and turn left over a stile in the corner.

Acton Bridge

Keep forward here, passing a telegraph pole, an oak tree and the hedge's end before turning right alongside it, walking towards the railway line – the west coast main line to London.

Cross the bridge over the railway, then, as you cross the long field in front of you, the houses of Acton Bridge village come into view. Climb over a stile by a gate and keep forward along a grassy track which drops down to the road.

3. Turn right and immediately left over a stile between a house and a bungalow, walking alongside a fence and hawthorn hedge to a stile. After this drop down the field ahead. In the distance you can see the River Weaver and the black-and-white swing bridge taking the A49 over it, towards which you are heading.

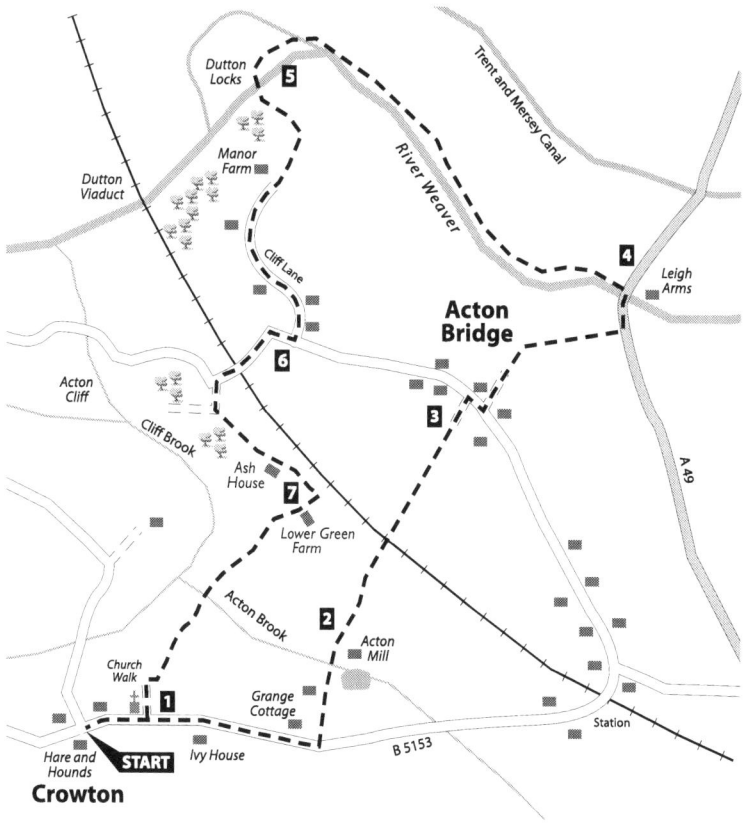

Drop steeply down the next field, keeping a sharp eye open for rabbits in the bank's sandy soil. Continue along a grassy path to another stile and bear slightly right across marshy ground to a kissing gate. Walk across the following field making for farm buildings, where you cross the bridge over the ditch before negotiating the stile beside the dog gate. After that a narrow path takes you to steps up to the A49. Turn left along the footpath here and cross the swing bridge.

Built in 1933, this spans two channels of the river here, pivoting on a central pontoon.

4. Once you have crossed the river turn left and drop down off the road to Acton Bridge Wharf, before continuing along the tarmac towpath (Dutton bridleway) towards Frodsham. Eventually, a fine white-painted timber bridge comes into view ahead and, turning left over it, you can see how the river was considerably straightened here, where cormorants are often seen fishing. You then reach Dutton Locks, founded in 1872, and now also an idyllic picnic spot.

Before reaching the lock-keepers' cottages you pass the impressive row of sluices which stretch across the old river course. The raising and lowering of their gates used to control the level of water in the main channel.

Traffic had increased so much towards the end of the 19th century that a lock to take larger vessels was built next to the existing one, which could take a steam packet towing three unpowered barges all at the same time. The heavy lock gates were operated by water turbines. Although still in place today under cast iron covers on the island between the locks, they were replaced by an electric system in 1979. Half-a-million gallons of water are lost during the operation of each lock.

In 2022 a mini hydro-electric power plant was installed here adjacent to Dutton Sluice by a company from Czechoslavakia. The massive red crane needed for this had to be brought in from Acton Wharf on a large pontoon. A separate pass allows for the safe migration of fish upstream.

From the locks you also get an excellent view of Dutton Viaduct. In use since 1837 it is the longest one on this main-line railway and its 20 equal red sandstone arches take trains high above the River Weaver.

Acton Bridge

A narrowboat glides under black-and-white Acton Bridge on the broad Weaver Navigation

Dutton Horse Bridge can be seen in front of the viaduct. Completed in 1919 this timber twin-span footbridge takes the towpath over a section of the Weaver Navigation.

5. Cross the river at the locks and walk uphill away from it, signposted to Acton Bridge. On reaching a field continue with the hedge on your left, climbing the stile at the end and turning right up the track to Manor Farm. A large, sandstone boulder helps to form a stile at the end of this and you keep ahead, first passing woodland on your left.

Continue forward along the road, eventually bearing left at a grassy triangle to pass several properties, including Weaver Holt with its ornately-patterned chimneys, eaves and walls. The name of this road is Cliff Lane which you discover when you come to a T-junction and turn right.

6. The road then drops down under the railway line and, just after it, take the first left turn uphill across the field. Continue

A narrow access bridge crosses an arm of the Weaver Navigation on the approach to Dutton Locks, near Crowton

through the farmyard at the far end, then along the lane passing Ash House to reach a T-junction.

7. Turn right here to Lower Green Farm. Then continue in the same direction on a bridleway, crossing Acton Brook on the way to Church Walk, then Station Road and the walk's end.

Crowton village is on your right and the Hare and Hounds is a popular local hostelry, well worth a visit.

22. Alvanley
Enjoy a saunter along the Sandstone Trail

Commonside, The Ridgeway, Sandstone Trail, Alvanley Cliff, Manley Road, The White Lion

---

Start: *Near Alvanley church. Map reference: SJ 497740.*

By Car: *Take the A56 east from Chester and, as you approach the outskirts of Helsby, turn right to Alvanley down Primrose Lane. As you enter the village turn right, then keep ahead past the school, church and White Lion inn. Park in a small layby on the right opposite Rose Cottage or ask to use the pub car park.*

Distance: *3 miles/6.5 kilometres.*

Duration: *Allow 2 hours.*

Difficulty: *Easy. Muddy in places.*

Food and Drink: *White Lion (01928 722949).*

Map: *OS 1:25,000 Explorer 267 Northwich & Delamere Forest.*

The walk

1. Notice the Georgian building of Church House Farm then cross the road and go down the footpath at the side of Rose Cottage.

On your left stands the church. Dating from 1860 and dedicated to St John the Evangelist, it has a tiny spire. An unusual custom used to take place here called 'roping'. A rope would prevent newly-married couples from leaving the church gate before they had paid a forfeit. This would then be used by the locals to drink their health in the White Lion!

When you are almost opposite Alvanley Cricket Club, founded in 1884 in its pleasant setting, go through a kissing gate into the next field. Continuing in the same direction, but now on the other side of the hedge, you eventually pass a pond and cross a field to reach the country lane known as Commonside.

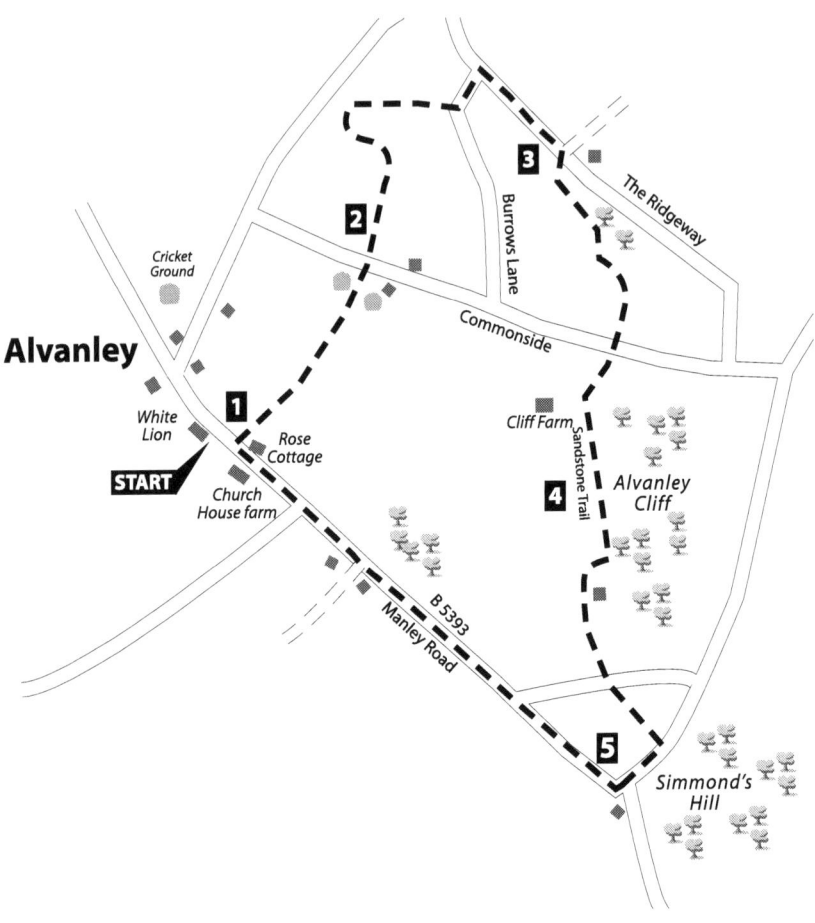

You used to have to negotiate a sturdy stile between stone pillars here but now there's a kissing gate.

2. Turn left, then right, along the footpath down the wood's edge, then continue along the side of a field.

Ahead, the industrial Mersey Valley is framed by the tree-covered Overton Hills.

Go through a wooden kissing gate at the field's end, then follow the hedge round to the left. The right-of-way skirts a

Alvanley

copse and continues to the holly hedge ahead, perhaps ablaze with bright red berries in winter.

Turn right alongside this and go right again in front of the bridge, signposted to Woodhouse Hill. You may find it muddy as you continue beside the stream to Burrows Lane, where you turn left, then turn right at the T-junction and walk uphill on The Ridgeway, an ancient route through the hills.

3. Opposite the holiday park's entrance turn right up steps. You have now joined the Sandstone Trail, which you follow for a considerable distance, walking towards Delamere Forest. Drop down through Ridgeway Wood and turn left, walking beside the stream until you cross a bridge out of this pretty oak woodland.

Walk up the field by the fence, following it round to the left until you go through a kisssing gate and bear left again to negotiate an area of mud and planks. Then keep forward on the path back to Commonside. Cross this and, as you walk uphill, Cliff Farm will come into view on the right.

An attractive building, typical of Cheshire with its black timbers and white infill, Cliff Farm is aptly named as the next part of the walk stays under Alvanley Cliff. You may see evidence of sandstone quarrying in the hillside and notice how the rocky outcrops have weathered. And the far-reaching views are superb.

4. Follow the cliff until you have to turn right at the end of the last field, then left, passing in front of timber-framed Austerson Old Hall.

This iconic Elizabethan timber-framed building was transported from Austerson, near Nantwich, in the 1970s, and was then painstakingly rebuilt in this attractive setting.

Turn left through a steel kissing gate into another field.

Sadly in some ways, this has replaced a unique stile with a very unusual construction, the top arm acting as a lever which made it easier to climb over.

Continue forward between fields to a country lane, which you cross, then go ahead, still on the Sandstone Trail as it drops

Fifteenth-century Austerson Old Hall was moved from near Nantwich and reconstructed below Alvanley Cliff in 1974

down to the next lane. Turn right along this with Simmond's Hill looming beside you.

5. Leaving the Sandstone Trail here turn right at the T-junction and walk back along Manley Road to your car.

You soon pass a milestone indicating that it is only a mile back to the village. And far over to your right stands Alvanley Hall. Constructed of red sandstone and with mullioned windows, much of it was built in the 17th century and it is surrounded by a variety of attractive gardens.

And before leaving this beautiful area you might like to relax for a while in The White Lion.

23. Delamere Forest

Forest pathways through shady woodland

Sandstone Trail, Linmere Lodge Visitor Centre, Harthill Bank, Hatchmere

Start: *Barnsbridge Gates car park. Map reference: SJ 542716.*

By Car: *Take the A51 east from Chester. Keep left onto the A54 towards Northwich. Turn left onto the B5393 to Ashton. Take the second right turn down Delamere Lane towards Hatchmere. Continue into Delamere Forest, passing Fox Howl outdoor education centre before turning right into Barnsbridge Gates car park.*

This landscaped gravel pit has become a bird lover's delight. Look out for wrens, nuthatches, jays, and many varieties of the tit family.

Distance: *6 miles/9.5 kilometres.*

Duration: *Allow 3 hours.*

Difficulty: *Easy-medium. One short climb out of the forest. A wet, boggy stretch after Hatchmere.*

Food and Drink: *Visitor Centre at Linmere Lodge (01606 889792); Carriers Inn (01928 788258) at Hatchmere.*

Map: *OS 1:25,000 Explorer 267 Northwich & Delamere Forest.*

The walk

1. From the end of the car park take the path that curves right, then turn left along the wide track of the Sandstone Trail. Keep right at the first junction and, following the distinctive Sandstone Trail markers, keep straight on at the next crossroads before bearing left at the next fork to the railway bridge.

Delamere Forest covers 4,000 acres/1,600 hectares of Cheshire today, but many centuries ago, when the Celts camped here, it was three times the size, covering the land from Nantwich to Helsby. In the Middle Ages it was made into the twin royal forests of Mara and Mondrem.

Delamere Forest

It seems incongruous to hear the hoot of a diesel in this quiet area but this is the Chester-Manchester line. Constructed in the 1870s, it was one of only a few lines built and owned by a committee – the Cheshire Lines Committee. It was also the last line to be brought into British Rail in 1947 – six months after the rest because of an oversight.

2. Keep ahead again at a junction of paths. Then leave the Sandstone Trail, bearing left where this continues, through a gap in a fence.

This is just before you reach Eddisbury Lodge, which takes its name from a hunting lodge situated here when the forest provided sport for the Norman nobility.

Continue along this wide path, uphill at first then passing seats and walking parallel with the railway line, but not re-crossing it, until you come to a gravel road and turn left.

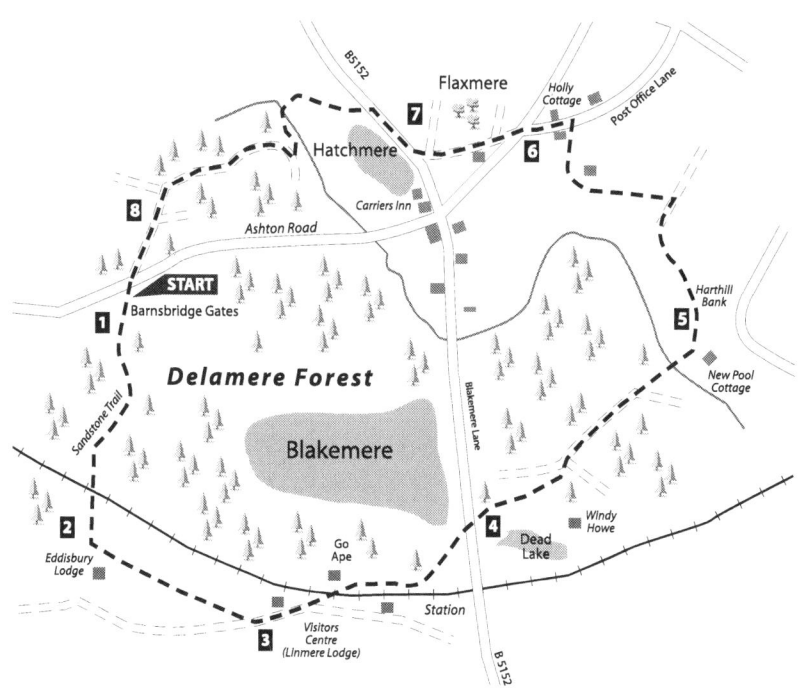

A ridge of hills rolls away nearby. The summit of Eddisbury Hill is the highest point, where there are the remains of an ancient fortress.

3. You soon arrive at Linmere Lodge visitor centre with its gift shop, cafe and toilets. After this you pass the old visitor centre buildings and continue along the road. Turn left to re-cross the railway, then go sharp right past the 'Go Ape' hut.

Advertised as a high wire forest adventure at tree-top height, it includes rope bridges, Tarzan swings and zip slides. So if you fancy shinning up trees on rope ladders and whizzing down a steel wire, then this is definitely for you!

Continue through the wood parallel with the railway line. The wide path soon narrows and winds between the trees, the leaf mould underfoot providing a soft surface for one's long-suffering feet!

4. Arriving at Blakemere Lane (B5152), cross over and continue through the enlarged Whitefield car park. You may spot Dead Lake shimmering through the trees and then glimpse Windy Howe perched on the hillside. Keep ahead through the carpark and clearings dominated by massive beech trees with far-reaching horizontal branches. These give way to younger beeches on either side of the path. The tangle of their shallow roots which often protrude above the surface are easy to trip over.

Keep ahead onto a wider track, signed as the Delamere Way, walking downhill to the right of a small reflective pond as silver birches drop away down the valley on your right. (There's a convenient picnic bench here.) Keep ahead at the first junction and climb up to another, where you bear slightly left up the Delamere Way and over the hill. This brings you out of the main forest and you continue forward between fields.

5. Just before you reach The Firs turn left through a gate, walking down a grassy track along the hillside known as Harthill Bank. Cross a small stream and a stile before bearing left uphill and continuing along the path to the facing hedge. Turn right here, continuing along the side of two fields until you are on the grassy track again, which leads down into a small valley.

Turn left along an almost hidden path before you reach the next gate and walk along the bottom of the field until you come to a steel gate into the next one. From here walk alongside the hawthorn hedge to a farm. Turn right down the farm track for a short distance before bearing left at the brick barn over a stile into a field. Walk up along the hedge to Post Office Lane where you turn left opposite Quavers Rest and Min Y Coed. (If you

The vast, recently flooded Blakemere lake, in the heart of Delamere Forest

miss the left turn continue ahead, turn left before some houses, then stay on this path to Post Office Lane, where you turn left to rejoin the route by Min Y Coed.)

6. At the fork continue ahead down the rough road to Hatchmere and, where this splits, go ahead again and bear left.

The area of land over to the right is called Flaxmere. It used to be a lake in the 13th century but is now reduced to a sunken moss.

The track finishes at a cottage inscribed with the date 1833 and the builder's initials. Keep ahead down a footpath here, then turn left down a dirt road as pretty reed-fringed Hatchmere comes into view.

There is a car park and toilets here, opposite the Carriers Inn which has been a pub for over 300 years. Important breeding birds on this acidic lake include great crested grebe, reed bunting and willow warbler.

7. Turn right along the B5152 and, where the mere ends, turn left along a clearly-marked path. Stay on this as it continues to the edge of the forest. Cross the bridge over one stream, then turn left alongside a second, next to a beaver enclosure.

This project was funded with £60.000 raised from fund-raising started in August 2020. The work was then completed in time for the release of a pair of beavers on 2nd November in that year.

Cross a wooden bridge and climb straight up the hill ahead to a broad forest 'ride'. Turn right along this, enjoying its grassy border and soft surface strewn with pine needles. Stay on this main track, ignoring any small enticing paths through the trees. Turn right when you come to a T-junction, dropping downhill before the track winds left again and takes you to the edge of the forest and a field on your right. (There's a seat at this point.)

8. Continue alongside the field, ignoring a stile on your right as you turn back into the forest. Finally, continue forward on a broad track and you will soon be back at Barnsbridge Gates.

24. Frodsham
Glorious views from Overton Hill

Beacon Hill, Sandstone Trail, Dunsdale Hollow, Woodhouse Hill Fort, Snidley Moor Wood, The Royalty, Riley Bank, Shepherd's Cottage

Start: *Small car park for the Sandstone Trail in Simons Lane near Beacon Hill. Map reference: SJ 519 766.*

By Car: *Take the A56 east from Chester. In the centre of Frodsham turn right onto the B5152. Turn right again towards Manley. Simons Lane is on the right signed for Frodsham Golf Club.*

Distance: *4 miles/6.5 kilometres.*

Duration: *Allow 2 hours.*

Difficulty: *Medium. Some ups and downs. Muddy in places.*

Food and Drink: *Plenty of eating places in Frodsham.*

Map: *OS 1:25,000 Explorer 267 Northwich & Delamere Forest.*

The walk

1. Turn right out of the carpark and, in around 80 metres or so, take the signed footpath on the left. The path soon opens out onto the golf course. Walk straight across this, taking care as you cross the fairways. At the far side, a well worn path takes you into the trees. Bear left down wooden steps and follow the path above the wooded valley of Dunsdale Hollow.

Steps have been constructed for an easy descent into the hollow, but for many years you had to scramble down a series of rock steps in the sandstone cliff known as 'Jacob's Ladder'. (You will be able to see this lower down when you look back.) Bear right after the steps to reach a path junction (Jacob's Ladder is on your right). Take the signed path to the left (Sandstone Trail) which crosses the back of the hollow.

Walks in West Cheshire and Wirral

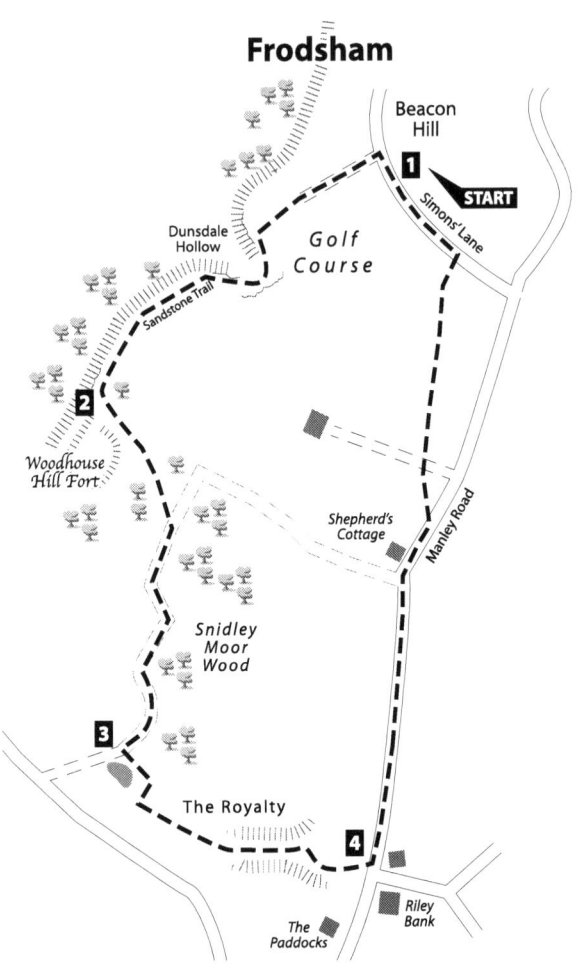

After a small footbridge, clamber up large sandstone steps, conveniently formed in the weathered rock and known locally as 'Abraham's Leap'. The Sandstone Trail then continues along the hilltop with the golf course on your left.

Keep ahead beyond the golf course, staying below the brow of the hill until you arrive at a viewpoint from a flat sandstone slab where there is also a bench.

The small town of Helsby can be seen nestling under the sandstone crag of its rugged hill and you can see how the drained marshland below is now used for agriculture. A seat has now been placed at this delightful picnic spot so that you can pick out landmarks at leisure. Liverpool's liver birds can be spotted as well as the Anglican and Catholic cathedrals behind Hale's lighthouse – the only one in Cheshire.

2. Continue along the Sandstone Trail, which swings left here up over Woodhouse Hill.

The wooded hilltop to the right is crowned by the scant remains of one of seven Iron Age forts sited along the sandstone ridge. All that is visible of the settlement is an earth mound, but the early families would have lived in huts, sheltered from the weather by the tree-covered hillside, and with a good vantage point from which to spot sudden danger.

With fields ahead, the path bends right beside a low sandstone wall (nothing to do with the hill-fort). With fields now on the left continue to a junction of paths. Follow the signed Sandstone Trail right, dropping gently downhill on a broad path, sandy underfoot. Evidence of rabbits, badgers and foxes can be found in the sandy banks as you continue along this broad track until the trees on your left finish.

3. Leave the Sandstone Trail for a signed path on the left at the end of the first field. Turn left through a kissing gate and walk up the side of the field.

The reed-fringed pool on the right has been formed as a blockage prevents water draining away naturally into the valley below.

At the top of the field turn right down a short track, then go left at its end through another kissing gate and continue below a bracken-strewn hillside known as 'The Royalty'. The valley you are now in is an unspoilt, natural delight. Towards its end, veer left and climb steeply up to a field, then continue along its edge to reach Manley Road.

Jacob's Ladder – now closed – was once the only route up and down

Dating from 1450, the house over to the right (now called 'The Paddocks') was once owned by a French abbot.

4. Turn left along the road. After passing 'Shepherd's Cottage', turn left over a stile into a field.

From here you have extensive views of the industrial belt along the Mersey valley out to the distant Liverpool skyline. The word 'Mersey' means 'river at the boundary' and this waterway used to form a natural boundary line between Lancashire and Cheshire.

Bear half-right across the field, walking towards the radio masts on the summit of Beacon Hill. Cross a farm lane, continuing ahead on an enclosed path with gardens on the right.

Views eventually also open up to the north-east, with Daresbury tower and Runcorn water tower being prominent landmarks.

At Simon's Lane turn left back to the carpark, which has information about the Sandstone Trail.

25. Kingsley

Watch out for herons on an unspoilt stretch of the River Weaver

Peel Hall, Hatley Farm, Beechmill, Bradley Orchard, Frodsham Cut, River Weaver, Catton Hall, Pike Lane

Start: *The Community Centre in Kingsley.*
Map reference: SJ 550748.

By Car: *Take the A56 from Chester. In the centre of Frodsham turn right onto the B5152. Turn left off this onto the B5153 to Kingsley. After passing the church, follow signs to the Community Centre, turning right onto Westbrook Road, then left down Smithy Lane, which bends left into the car park.*

Distance: *6 miles/9.5 kilometres.*

Duration: *Allow 3 hours.*

Difficulty: *Easy. Muddy in places.*

Food and Drink: *Lady Heyes Craft Centre (Tea room: 01928 788539); The Red Bull, Kingsley (01928 787121).*

Map: *OS 1:25,000 Explorer 267 Northwich & Delamere Forest.*

The walk

1. Walk through the gap in the hedge to the Co-op and the Horseshoe Garage, then turn left back along the B5153. Continue past the church and, part-way up the slope, steep sandstone steps and a metal kissing gate on the right lead into a field.

Keep the hedge on your right and follow it round until you cross a broken stile into the next field. (It can be very muddy here.) Carry on in the same direction with the land falling away to give a wide sweeping view, then drop down out of this field onto a tarmac drive which leads to a lane. Turn slightly right along this, then left over another stile.

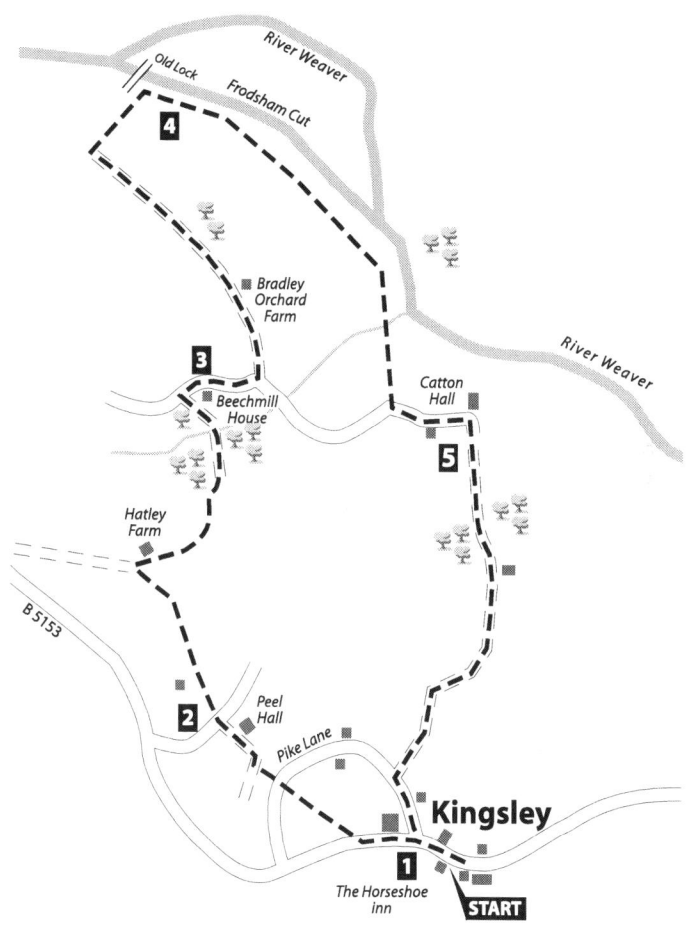

There are tracks to either side but you go straight down to cross a sturdy bridge over the stream. This is a pretty valley, with the brook babbling below as you continue over a stile, then along the path to another and, when you come to a grassy track, turn right uphill.

At the end of this go over a stile into a field and, keeping the hedge, then a brick wall with sandstone coping-stones, on your right, continue to Peel Hall – a farmhouse built on the site of a much older moated grange. Leave the field via a stile and turn left away from the buildings along the farm lane.

2. When you reach a T-junction cross the lane and go down the track opposite, which takes you first along the side of a field, then across it. Keeping the hedge on your left, continue along the edge of the next field until you leave it over a stile, to the left of Hatley Farm.

Over to the left, cottages on the outskirts of Frodsham nestle under the hillside and Lady Heyes Craft Centre is well worth a visit.

Turn right towards the farm and make your way through the farmyard, continuing onto a rough track, then dropping down the field keeping the hedge on your right. Cross the stile into the next field and turn right, following the fence down to a footpath sign and stile. Do not go over this but turn left, now walking straight across the field to a signpost under oak trees at the far side.

From here cross a very muddy area and continue in the same direction to reach a track bordered by tall trees and a profusion of wildflowers. After crossing the stream in its steep valley, where a waterfall drops noisily away, you soon come to Beechmill House – built on the site of the original mill.

3. Walk down the drive and turn right onto a country lane, dropping downhill until, almost at the bottom, you turn left along a stony track. On reaching Bradley Orchard Farm, a dirt track continues ahead, to the left of the farmhouse, then uphill.

The railway viaduct and the M56 span the wide valley ahead – feats of engineering from different centuries.

The hillside drops away steeply beside you and, on reaching a junction, take the left fork, to continue in the same direction, following the track over the next field. Immediately beyond a splendid mixed hedgerow, with trees at its end, make a right-angled turn to drop down alongside these. At their end keep straight ahead over a stile, crossing a field to another stile, beyond which a solitary bench constitutes the remains of a picnic area at Frodsham Lock. Turn right here and walk on the towpath alongside Frodsham Cut.

The river was tidal here and boats carrying salt from the works further upstream were often delayed. This expensive improvement, with a lock and sluices, was built in 1781 to provide a deeper channel. The large weir over to the left was built at the same time, so that all traffic had to use the cut and pay a toll. However, the construction of the Weston Canal in 1810, on the far side of the natural river, provided an alternative route and the cut was finally closed to navigation in 1955. Today, although overgrown and neglected it is a haven for wildlife. Look out for herons, families of swans and large flocks of geese.

4. Cross two stiles where a bridge, so low that a punt could scarcely pass under it, crosses the water. When the cut ends continue beside the River Weaver for some distance, in summer enjoying the wildflowers which stud the river banks, often muddy in winter.

Leave the river where it bears left at the end of a long field. Here the path turns right, joining a track used by quad bikers, with the hedge on your right. Continue up this, walking straight ahead to pass by a steel kissing gate, then up the side of a field to a

Swans doze and preen on a quiet stretch of the River Weaver near Kingsley

Rusting mechanisms and a derelict sluice are all that remain of Frodsham Lock on the Weaver Navigation, near Kingsley

country lane. Turn left here towards Catton Hall, now surrounded by several other dwellings.

Before the river was navigable, it could be crossed by a ford here.

5. Approaching the hall, veer right towards new houses, then make a right-angled turn up a track to a wood. Walk through this and stay on the track as Kingsley church comes into view ahead and you eventually turn left onto Pike Lane. Pass Church Cottage, then turn left at the lychgate to return to the start or to seek out the Red Bull for welcome refreshment.

Standing high above the road, and dedicated to St John the Evangelist, Kingsley's beautiful little church was built in locally quarried red sandstone. Designed by Sir Gilbert Scott, it was consecrated in 1851. The spire which tops the small tower is lit by tiny dormer windows and inside is a handsome iron screen.

26. Primrosehill Wood

Deciduous and evergreen woodland, and far-reaching views from the Sandstone Trail

Primrosehill Wood, Tirley Garth, Utkinton, Sandstone Trail, Primrosehill Wood, Stoney Lane

Start: *Lay-by on Stoney Lane, Delamere. Map reference: SJ 553683.*

By Car: *Take the A51 from Chester, turning left at Tarvin onto the A54. Where the A556 and A54 split, bear right heading towards Winsford. Turn left in 800 metres and park in a lay-by on the right.*

Distance: 5½ miles/9 kilometres.

Duration: *Allow 3 hours.*

Difficulty: *One or two uphill sections. Muddy in places.*

Food and Drink: *Abbeywood Gardens Cafe (01606 889477) on the A556 is 1 km to the east of the starting point (towards Delamere).*

Map: *OS 1:25,000 Explorer 267 Northwich & Delamere Forest.*

The walk

1. Return to the A54 and turn left along the pavement. At footpath signs to left and right, cross over with care and walk down the side of a long field. Climb the stile and keep ahead again, following the wood's edge uphill, beside smooth-boled beech.

Both now and at the end of the walk you are in Primrosehill Wood. This large, detached segment of Delamere Forest is a mixture of Scots and Corsican pine, with deciduous trees around its perimeter in which squirrels build their dreys, and you may see willow warbler, chiffchaff, treecreeper or nuthatch. The carpet of leaf mould and leaves make the ground soft underfoot and, on a clear day, as you climb higher you will be rewarded with views over to the Pennines.

Drop down the other side of the hill and, after crossing a stream, the path ascends again beside a wire fence – a steep pull up to a stile and Tirley Lane.

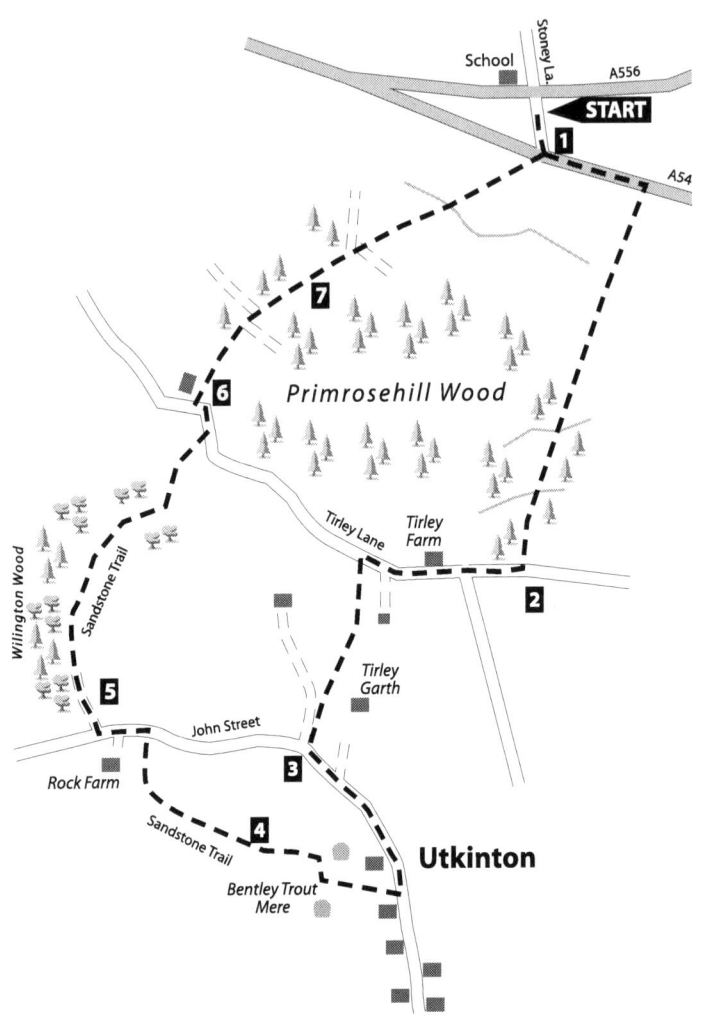

2. Turn right, then keep ahead at the crossroads towards Kelsall, passing Tirley Farm. Just past the back entrance to Tirley Garth, with its lodge, turn left down a footpath signposted to John Street. Follow blue arrows all the way down this pretty valley, then, after going through a gate, continue ahead down a farm road to John Street.

3. Turn left here, passing the impressive front entrance to Tirley Garth with its sandstone steps and pillars, and you soon arrive at Utkinton.

Built in 1907, the large country house on the Tirley Garth estate is shielded from view but the building has an interesting history. It was bought by Mersey Television (founded by Phil Redmond and now know as Lime Pictures) in 2002. So perhaps the internal cloisters now provide the set for many a production.

Turn right down a snicket just before Boundary Cottage and continue beside an unusual wall structure. Keep ahead down the side of a field, then ahead again between two fishing pools before leaving this sheltered spot by a stile.

In 2021 this path was blocked by a landslide but this was soon repaired and a smart new bridge installed.

Turn right and enjoy extensive views as you walk up the side of the field. Beeston Castle comes into view as you stay beside

Spring flowers decorate the high banks of sunken green Sandy Lane, on the Sandstone Trail, near Willington

the hedge, then cross stiles and a track into the next field. You have now joined the Sandstone Trail.

4. Continue in the same direction, with the Cheshire Plain resembling an intricately patterned quilt as it spreads out as far as the Welsh foothills. At the field's end turn right over a stile and walk to the road. Notice the Sandstone Trail milestone as you turn left towards Rock Farm with its brick-built barn.

5. As the road starts to drop downhill turn right up a sandy bridleway – aptly named Sandy Lane – following the Sandstone Trail towards Delamere. The evergreen strip of Willington Wood is a field's width away as you walk through stretches of soft sand and, after passing sandstone outcrops in a coppice of huge beech trees and a fine horse chestnut, the path may become muddy as a spring surfaces here.

Walk up a sunken path between banks topped by hawthorn – a typical feature of the Cheshire countryside. Turn left along Tirley Lane for a few yards, then right at a sharp corner to follow the Sandstone Trail marker towards Delamere Forest once more.

6. Continue down the path alongside what used to be the popular Summer Trees Tearoom, then keep ahead along the field's edge towards the wide sweep of Primrosehill. Drop down the next field and, towards the end of it, go through the steel kissing gate on your right. From here continue in the same direction at first, then veer right, leaving the Sandstone Trail and dropping down to exit by a wooden stile.

7. Go straight ahead through the forest, crossing over a flint road and keeping forward until you leave it through a metal kissing gate. Walk forward to a second kissing gate, then cross the facing field diagonally right, dropping down into the dip, then climbing up to the kissing gate ahead. Cross the track here and continue in the same direction, past a pylon, then an oak and brambles on your right, to two metal kissing gates and the A54. Cross this busy road with care and walk up Stoney Lane back to your car.

27. Burton

Along the old shoreline and through the pretty village of Burton

Station Road, Burton village, Burton Wood, Ness Gardens, Orchard House, Ness, Dee estuary

Start: *By the Dee estuary at Burton. Map reference: SJ 301747.*

By Car: *Take the A540 towards Heswall. Turn left to Burton down Mudhouse Lane and keep left through Burton. At the end of the village bear left down Station Road. There are several parking places alongside the Dee estuary.*

Distance: *5 miles/8 kilometres.*

Duration: *Allow 2 to 3 hours.*

Difficulty: *Easy.*

Food and Drink: *The Wheatsheaf in Ness. Open all day every day. Home-cooked food all day on Sundays, at lunchtime and in the evening on all other days. (0151 336 6336). Cafe at Ness Botanic Gardens (0151 353 0123). Tea garden at Denhall House Farm.*

Map: *OS 1:25,000 Explorer 266 Wirral & Chester.*

The walk

1. Walk back to Burton up Station Road.

A bridge crosses the Wrexham to Bidston railway line here and, although Burton Point station is closed, you can still see the platform, signal box and station master's house with its attractive brickwork, ornate eaves and chimney.

On the right Burton Point Farm is owned by the RSPB and has a visitors' centre, and the Dovecote Nurseries have been run by the same family since before the 2nd World War.

Then look out for the pretty copse – a peaceful spot where steps lead down to seats. The spring which surfaces here was originally

The church of St Nicholas, Burton, with its one-handed clockface

named Patrick's Well, but by the 19th century it had become known as Hampston's Well, after a family that had lived in Burton since the 16th century.

The water here had possibly first served Iron Age settlements at Burton Point, followed by Anglo-Saxons living in Burton around AD 900. Later Manor Court records frequently mention that constables cleaned it each year and all the able-bodied men of Burton were required to help or be fined sixpence. No clothes' washing was allowed either.

2. Bear right into Burton.

Burton Manor is now an adult training college but was once the home of Henry Neville Gradstone. Son of the Liberal prime minister, he remodelled the hall and planted many trees to provide firewood and cover for pheasant rearing.

Burton originated as a small fishing and farming community, the people settling here because the high land was surrounded by good *ploughing soil and there were springs of fresh water. In the 13th century it developed further as a port trading with Ireland, which flourished until the River Dee silted up four centuries later.*

Notice that many of Burton's red sandstone cottages are built into the bedrock above the sloping village street. Thatched Barn End may be the oldest property, built around 1450.

At Rake Corner turn left. Keep ahead up steps, then turn right, walking through Burton Wood above the village.

You soon pass the two Quakers' Graves. One dated 1663, they lie side by side, relics from a time when Quakers were thought to have 'an

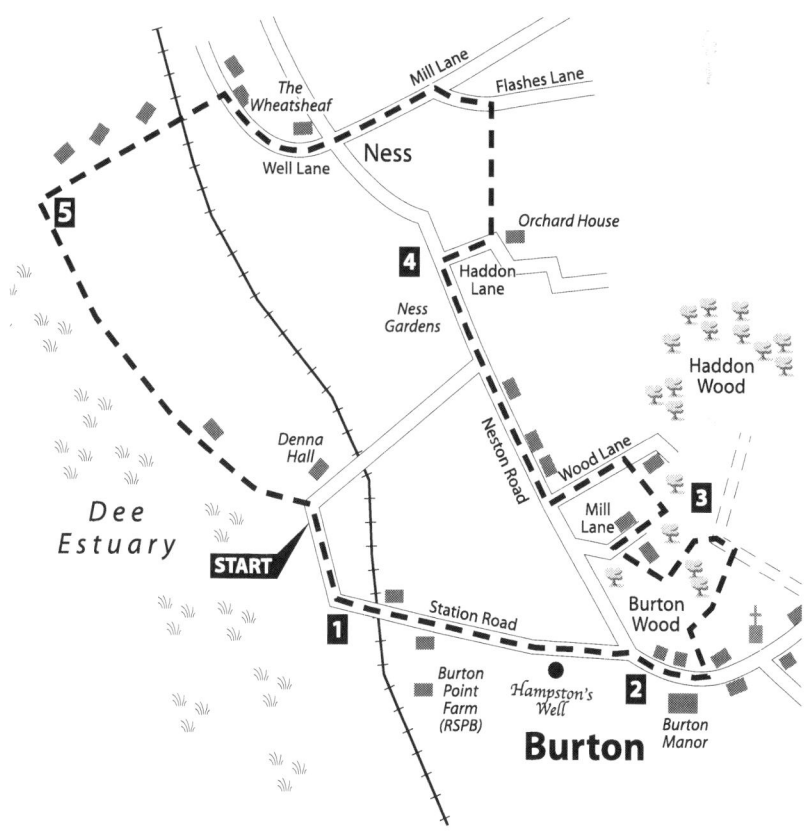

active spirit of evil' and so were buried in unconsecrated ground. Today they are preserved as a tribute to these men and women who lived a courageous life in difficult times.

The church tower soon comes into view and you may like to deviate right for a few yards to visit the church.

Facing the village, high up on the tower of St Nicholas' church is an unusual one-handed clockface. The interior has a double nave and an ancient font that looks like two big drums one above the other. The Jacobean communion rails are said to be the oldest in Cheshire and, in a showcase, is a Bible dating from the time of Elizabeth I and still attached to a piece of old chain.

From where you detoured right, turn left to continue on a narrow path to an iron kissing gate. Then turn left up a tarmac lane and keep ahead through another kissing gate onto National Trust land.

Burton Wood covers 24 acres of mature woodland, mainly deciduous except for some towering Scots pine. Giant horse and sweet chestnuts, oak and beech mix with rowan, hawthorn and the invasive but colourful rhododendron. Damp and decaying vegetation provide ideal conditions for fungi such as stinkhorn, shaggy inkcap and Jew's ear.

Sweet-scented plants thrive, for example lady's smock, wood sorrel and foxglove. Snowdrops herald spring, followed by wild hyacinths and bluebells. Birdlife is prolific, with green and greater spotted woodpeckers, tawny and little owls, jays, goldcrests and an occasional breeding pair of wood warblers. And, late in the day, pipistrelle bats flit among the trees.

3. Walk forward through the wood along a wide path, which bears left, then right parallel to a low fence. Exit by an iron kissing gate and turn right up Mill Lane. Continue along a snicket bordering a property called 'Mill Wood'.

In its grounds you pass the ivy-covered ruins of an old mill. This pegmill once stood on top of a bare hillside with panoramic views. In the 1980s its crumbling walls showed a datestone of 1771 and the initials RO, which referred to the miller, Robert Oliver.

Turn left down through the wood, then left again down Wood Lane to Neston Road. Cross over with care and turn right along the pavement for about 900 yards. At Ness Gardens cross over and continue on the opposite footpath.

4. Just past the main entrance turn right down Haddon Lane and, at Orchard House, turn left along a path. At a junction turn left, keeping ahead along Flashes Lane before turning left again down Mill Lane into Ness.

Reaching Neston Road again, notice the Wheatsheaf's traditional inn sign depicting a cornfield at harvest time. Then continue ahead, leaving the village down Well Lane. Opposite Willow Croft and New Heys turn left and follow the footpath all the way down to the Dee estuary.

5. Here, turn left again alongside the marshes, with splendid views over the silted up Dee estuary to the Welsh hills.

Along here Marsh Cottage used to be two dwellings and at one time high tides used to sweep through the gardens.

As you approach the grounds of Denna Hall, the remnants of stained glass in the arched windows of a sandstone tower indicate that it was once perhaps a private chapel. You then have a view of the house and its stone balcony. The original building dated back to before 1650 when plague struck at least one of the occupants.

John Summers and his wife lived there in the 1930s. She was the sister of George Mallory, the mountaineer who died on Everest. His family founded the steelworks at Shotton. In 1936 the house became Fen Hall in a film and many scenes were shot locally.

After passing Denhall House Farm on your left you soon reach your car at the end of the sandstone wall.

The land on your left is scheduled as an ancient monument. From the 13th century to the 16th the hospital of St Andrew there ministered to the poor and shipwrecked, often from Ireland.

In spring and autumn thousands of migratory birds can be seen feeding on the marshes and mudflats here.

28. Christleton

A common, a canal and a village church

Little Heath Common, Rake Lane, Brown Heath Road, Shropshire Union Canal, Christleton and Littleton

Start: *Car park at Little Heath Common by the children's play area. Map reference: SJ 443660.*

By Car: *Take the A41 from Chester, then turn left to Christleton. (This pretty village is only two miles from Chester and wealthy merchants trading in the city built themselves houses here. You enter the village on Pepper Street, where many of the houses are Georgian. On your left, look out for a gazebo built into the walls of Christleton Hall and Christleton House. These towers, erected in the garden walls of big houses, enabled ladies to see what was going on outside.)*

Turn left at the church into Little Heath Road and turn right as you come to a pretty pool, fringed by reeds. Continue past this to an open area for parking, adjacent to a children's playground and sports field.

Distance: *4 miles/6.5 kilometres.*

Duration: *Allow 2 hours.*

Difficulty: *Easy.*

Food and Drink: *Ring o' Bells (01244 335422) in Christleton.*

Map: *OS 1:25,000 Explorer 266 Wirral & Chester.*

The walk

1. Walk back to the car park's entrance and turn left down a track, then alongside a field. Walk down the side of this with the hedge on your right and go through a gap into the next field. Turn left here and follow the hedge round the field until you reach the remains of a stile set in sandstone pillars – a feature of this area although, sadly, many of the struts are now missing from them. Walk down the long side of the next rectangular field and exit from it via a further stile or through a gap.

Turn right beside the pond to a seat dedicated to John David Salter 1940-2001. Then continue on a path through open areas, bearing right before the road, but parallel with it, to a junction.

2. From here walk ahead down Rake Lane, a continuation of Stamford Lane, towards Waverton, passing aptly named White Gate Farm, then old and new cottages, before entering Brown Heath Road at a crossroads. Continue along this until, just before the 30mph sign, you turn right down a track.

You have now joined the Baker Way, a long distance route of 14 miles, from Chester to Delamere Forest.

Pass through a small metal gate and veer right past a pond fringed by hawthorn and willow. A 'V'-shape in the fence beside

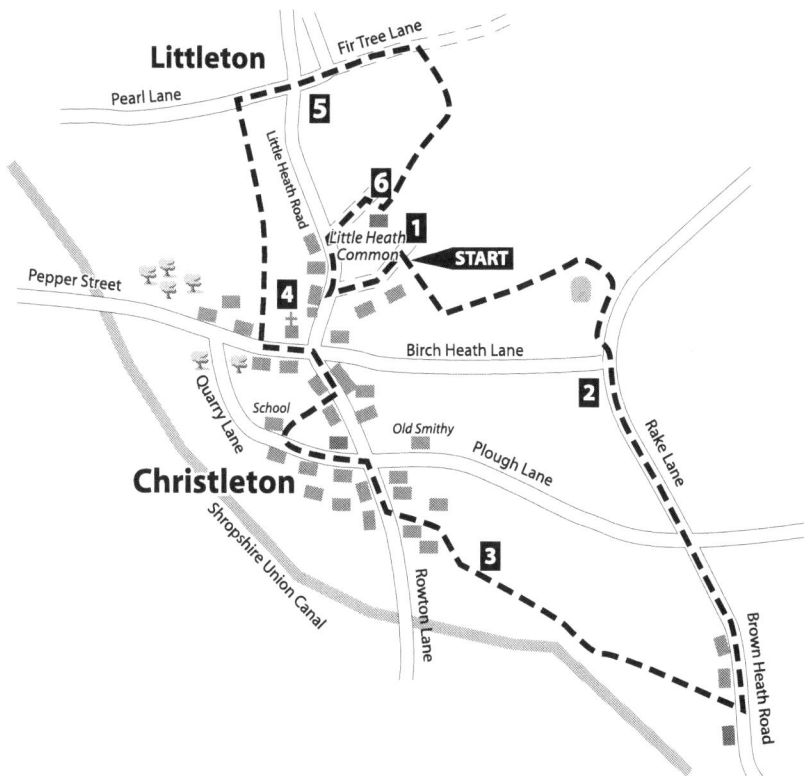

a gate then allows access into the next field. Continue with the hedge on your right to a steel kissing gate in the far corner. From here climb up onto the bank of the Shropshire Union Canal and turn right along it.

You are now following the canal's Chester branch which runs from Barbridge Junction, passes Bunbury and Beeston, then starts its drop down to Chester at Christleton. Probably the first hire cruisers on the canal system were started from a boatyard here way back in 1935, when the price of a 2-berth boat was £4 a week.

3. For most of the way this path is narrow and can be muddy. At its end leave the canal, veering over the field to a kissing gate. Cross straight over the next field to another, then walk down a snicket with a grassy mound on your left. At the end of this continue forward down Skips Lane.

Looking across reed-fringed Christleton Pool to the black-and-white Victorian almshouses

Turn right along Rowton Bridge Road to a crossroads where you turn left down Quarry Lane.

The first pair of houses on your left were once the village school for girls. The boys were taught in the village hall.

Continue on this road, noting the police sign high up in the stonework of a house on the right, before you turn right down a footpath just before the primary school. At the end of this turn left, passing a general store, pretty cottages and the Ring o' Bells, an old coaching inn, before arriving at the church and the village green in the centre of Christleton.

On the triangle here is the old pumphouse. Built in 1886 and carved from wood on a sandstone base, unusually its pump is placed outside the building. The low Manor House next to the church has walls of local brick and a Tudor porch. The white-painted milestone in the wall near it has distances to the local villages – Hoole, Rowton, Littleton and Piper's Ash and, in place of the apostrophe, there's a comma!

St James' church is worth visiting. A place of worship has stood on this site for well over 1000 years. In fact Christleton, 'the place of the Christians', gets its name from those early worshippers. The oldest part of the present church is the 15th century sandstone tower. Gargoyles hang off the four corners below the high parapet, topped by a square lantern and a cockerel weather vane. Dating only back to 1888, the gilt clock completes the picture.

The rest of the church is Victorian and the architect William Butterfield incorporated mathematical shapes, colourful tiles, coral limestone and seasoned oak in its decoration and furnishings to enhance this beautiful building. Charles Kempe designed most of the stained glass windows, a 'pelican' is a remnant from the 1737 building, there is a Bible box, and a unique oak font cover features 'tools of self reliance'. In the churchyard notice the war memorial and a cross, erected in memory of Canon Lionel Garnett, Rector here from 1869 to 1911.

4. Facing the church, turn left along Pepper Street and, at the churchyard's end, turn right along the footpath to Littleton. After a kissing gate walk over a field.

On your left you can glimpse the old wall around the 18th century Christleton Hall – now a law school dwarfed by modern extensions.

Continue on this well-trodden path alongside fields, noting the variety of trees – silver birch, rowan, ash, crab apple, sycamore and cherry. Turn right at Pearl Lane, passing several gnarled old oaks as you come to the outskirts of Littleton.

5. At the crossroads go ahead down Littleton Lane, passing Orchard House with its massive chimney breast before bearing right down Fir Tree Lane. Keep forward on a rough track, then turn right at a junction of paths down the side of a field, with splendid views. Then turn right at the far side of two oaks to cross the field.

6. Keep forward at the remains of a stile into the next field, then keep the hedge on your right all the way round to Pitts Cottage, a stile's stone pillars and an access road. Turn right along this, passing two mossy stones, one once engraved with a sheaf of wheat, the other with a portcullis.

Turn left down Little Heath Road to return to Little Heath Common with its attractive pool. From here turn left, then left again as you pass the bungalow with the stork weather vane. You then pass the black-and-white almshouses, built in the 19th century, that face the pool, as you return to your car.

Little Heath Common was formed from excavating clay which, in the 18th century, was used as gravel on roads, and marl was spread on fields to improve soil quality. The pool here was the largest pit formed from this. Today only one other remains, the rest having been filled in.

The area is a wildlife haven and a credit to the local community. Herons feed here, flying from the large heronry at Eaton Hall where they nest. Weeping willows provide shade and bullrushes (reedmace) line the banks, together with reed sweetgrass and yellow flag iris. Amphibious bistort grows in shallow areas, coots, moorhens and many other birds, bob about on the water, and roach and tench thrive in it. It's an idyllic spot.

29. Thornton Hough

Follow in Lord Lever's footsteps

Brimstage Hall, Thornton Common Road, Thornton Hough, Brimstage Road

Start: *Brimstage Hall Craft Centre. Map reference: SJ 304827.*

By Car: *Take the M53 west from Ellesmere Port. Exit at Junction 4 and take the A5137 towards Heswall. In Brimstage, turn left into Brimstage Craft Centre's car park.*

Distance: *3 miles/5 kilometres.*

Duration: *Allow 1 to 2 hours.*

Difficulty: *Easy.*

Food and Drink: *The Country Mouse Restaurant (0151 342 5382) in Brimstage Craft Centre. In Thornton Hough The Turret Tea Rooms are shut on Sundays (0151 336 3719); The Seven Stars inn (0151 336 4574) serves food all day, every day.*

Map: *OS 1:25,000 Explorer 266 Wirral & Chester.*

The walk

1. Walk back past the entrance to Brimstage Hall.

Now a private residence, this dates back to turbulent, medieval times, when its peel tower provided a refuge for villagers. Arrow slits and the machiolated roof remain. From the latter boiling water was poured onto attackers and the clockwise spiral stairs allowed a retreating defender free use of his sword arm. Faint traces of the moat are also still visible in the adjacent fields.

Continue on the road to the old iron black-and-white signpost – a feature of Wirral. Turn right here to Thornton Hough, through a metal kissing gate. Walk down the field's side, cross stiles and a track, then veer left to another kissing gate. Continue down the side of the next two fields, with the hedge first on your left, then your right.

All Saints' Church, Thornton Hough, framed by its wooden lychgate

Cross a carriage drive here and walk forward over the following field on a clearly defined path. At the far end turn left down a hedged path between fields to the end of another tree-lined drive. Keep forward to pass its end, then set off down a stony track, which immediately veers right. Follow this until footpaths leave it on either side and you turn right through a kissing gate.

2. Walk down the side of two fields with the hedge on your left, then keep in the same direction on a clearly defined path over a third. Go through the gate at the far end and turn left to Thornton Common Road, passing sandstone Crofts Bank Cottages on your left. Cross with care and turn right on the pavement.

At the end of the 19th century much of Thornton Hough was rebuilt by William Hesketh Lever, the founder of the Lever soap factory at Port Sunlight. The half-timbered cottages here were modelled on that village and he also built several large houses for members of his family. In 1906 he built St George's United Reform Church on the village green. Of Norman style and extensively decorated inside with stone carving, its tower is low in order not to detract from the Anglican church.

By 1870, All Saints parish church and vicarage had been built by Joseph Hirst, a West Yorkshire textile manufacturer from Huddersfield. Unusually, its tall steeple has five clock faces, the fifth added so that he could see the time from his bedroom window in Thornton House. The

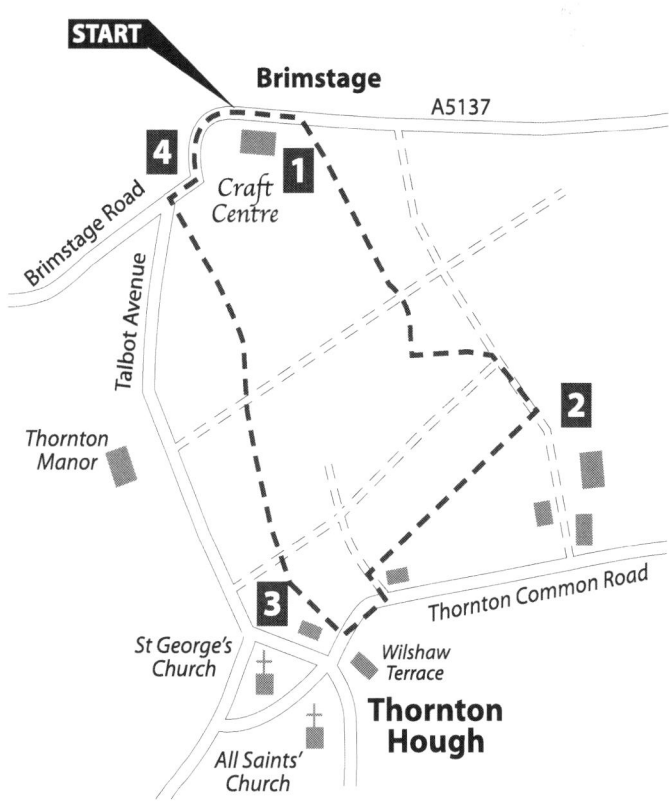

church stands behind Wilshaw Terrace, which he also built, and the Turret Tea Rooms used to be the village store and post office. Notice its 1870 datestone.

3. Turn right down a broad track behind the primary school – erected in 1905 by Lord Leverhulme. This soon becomes a tarmac lane, then, at another carriage drive, turn right and immediately left down a path between fields. Go through the kissing gate at its end and continue along the field side, with the hedge on your right. (Note the sandstone blocks, originally intended to give you a leg up before kissing gates replaced the stiles.)

Continue down the side of the next field, with the hedge on your left, towards a stand of Scots pine and a kissing gate. The path then crosses straight over the third field to an old iron kissing gate. Cross the grassy drive here, go through another kissing gate and cross the field veering slightly right to a final kissing gate.

Thornton Manor, now an upmarket hotel, is over to your left. Built in the 1840s, it became the home of the Lever family in 1888, and continued to be so until Lord Leverhulme, last of the line, died in 2000. He is buried in All Saints' churchyard.

Walk down the side of the next field with the hedge on your right, to a stile in it part-way along. Then continue on a sheltered path between fields all the way to Talbot Avenue, where you turn right, then right again along Brimstage Road.

4. Where this turns sharp left, go right through a gap under an oak. Walk along the field side, with the fence on your left, to another gap which takes you back into the car park.

30. Thurstaston

A common, a country park, a wood, and the Wirral Way

Wirral Way, The Dungeon, Thurstaston village and common, Royden Country Park, Stapledon Wood, Caldy, Wirral Way

Start: *Wirral Way car park. Map reference: SJ 239834.*

By Car: *Take the A540 from Heswall towards West Kirby. Approaching Thurstaston, turn left down Station Road, then left at the far end into the visitors' centre car park.*

Distance: *7 miles/11 kilometres.*

Duration: *Allow 3 to 4 hours.*

Difficulty: *One or two inclines. Muddy in places.*

Food and Drink: *The Cottage Loaf in Thurstaston (0151 6482837) serves food all day.*

Map: *OS 1:25,000 Explorer 266 Wirral & Chester.*

The walk

1. Turn left along the Wirral Way (towards Heswall) enjoying sweeping views over the silted Dee estuary to North Wales. Continue under the echoing, brick Dungeon Bridge, then take the next left turn, signposted to The Dungeon. Walk up the fenced-in path between fields, then turn left over the stream as you enter woodland – or you may first like to detour ahead to investigate the caves.

In this instance the name Dungeon simply means a dell. Carved out by its stream, this steep-sided ravine and ancient oak woodland contains Wirral's only natural waterfall.

Ascend steps to a viewpoint, from which you can see the Point of Ayr lighthouse in Wales. Then turn right, ascending with the waterfall and caves below. Keep right above the stream, then re-cross it and continue through deciduous woodland until you reach a junction and turn left towards Thurstaston. Follow the path between fields, with the church spire pointing the way ahead, all the way to Thurstaston village.

The name Thurstaston is of Viking origin and the red sandstone church, dedicated to St Bartholomew, is the third built on this site. Nothing remains of the first Norman building but the tower of the second, demolished in the 19th century, still stands in the churchyard.

After passing the church turn right up Station Road. Cross over before the roundabout and turn left along Telegraph Road, passing the Cottage Loaf inn before turning right along the path onto Thurstaston Common.

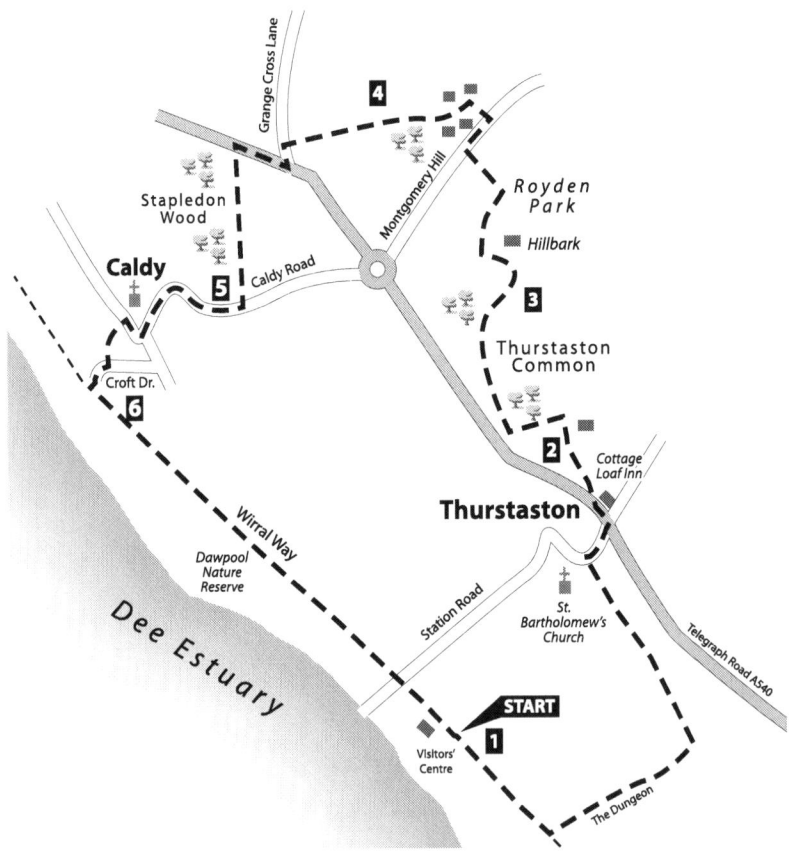

Walkers out for a stroll on Thurstaston Common

2. Keep right at the first fork to pass the village school's new buildings then, immediately after The Old School House, turn left up the path to the OS trig. point and the sandstone pillar.

From here you have spectacular views south over the Dee estuary to the Welsh hills. Then, more locally, look for the globe-topped column on Caldy Hill, Hoylake, and Leesowe lighthouse. And particularly prominent in Liverpool are the Anglican cathedral and the airport.

Bear right, admiring the view and following the ridge along on sandstone outcrops until you drop down through flaming yellow gorse, then a silver birch and oak woodland. At a junction of paths go ahead through a wall gap into Royden Country Park. Turn right, then veer left to open parkland.

Once farmland, in the 19th century Royden became a large country estate. However, since 1961 it has been a public open space which, together with Thurstaston Common, comprises almost 250 acres of woods, heath and parkland.

3. Turn right here to have the best view of Hill Bark.

This splendid half-timbered mock Tudor mansion, with its massive chimney pots, was built on Bidston Hill in 1891 for a wealthy soap manufacturer, R W Hudson, and was named Bidston Court. In 1931 it was moved, brick by brick, to its present position and was renamed Hillbark. Today it is a luxury hotel.

Turn left, taking the path in front of the hotel. Stay on this, bearing right all the way to the wood's edge, where you turn left on a broad ride which leads to a road – Montgomery Hill.

Cross over and turn right here, then left down the private road to Birch Heys. Keep left behind the houses, ignoring the footpath to Grange. Pass the entrance to Royden Manor, Birch House, the Birch Heys Farm complex and several other attractive sandstone properties.

4. At the end of the lane turn right, then left along a grassy track, passing Scots pine on the way to a substantial sandstone stile. Drop down the long field here, with the hedge on your right and enjoy the splendid views over to the Welsh hills. Leave the field by a stile, where it may be muddy, and continue on a path between fence and hedge, then go down an alleyway to another stile and Grange Cross Lane.

Turn left, then cross over and turn right along Telegraph Road. After Sylvan Lea (No. 50), turn left through a gap in the sandstone wall. Ascend steps, then keep left, following the small, narrow path along the edge of Stapledon Wood until you come to a facing fence and turn left down sandstone steps. Then continue forward down to Caldy Road.

Stapledon Wood was named after Olaf Stapledon, a local philosopher and writer of science fiction. This attractive mixed woodland of oak, sweet chestnut, beech, ash and elm is enhanced in spring by a mass of daffodils, then bluebells. It is also rich in birdlife – woodpecker, tree creeper, nuthatch, spotted and pied flycatcher, and many warblers.

The mock Tudor mansion of Hill Bark with its plethora of chimney pots

5. Turn right and walk into Caldy village.

Nestling beneath the wooded slopes of Caldy Hill, until 1832 the village consisted of a few fishermen's huts and small cottages. At that time R W Barton, a Manchester businessman, set about improving it by building the red sandstone dwellings with black-and-white timberwork you see today.

Continue round the corner past the church to a sandstone cross, where you bear left down a path through trees. Then turn right onto Croft Drive and continue down to the Wirral Way.

6. Turn left along this. To relieve the monotony, you can detour right into Dawpool Nature Reserve, which has a bench where you can rest and admire the view, before bearing left along a grassy path parallel with the Wirral Way, then back onto it. Eventually you reach May Kirby Bridge and what was the station platform and return to whichever car park you have used.

About the Author

Jen Darling lived in Cheshire with her husband for over 36 years, brought up four children there and taught in primary schools until 1986. Published in 1988, *West Cheshire Walks* was the first book she wrote.

Having worked for a local printer and found that she enjoyed the typesetting and design aspects of the work, in 1991 she founded her own company, *Alfresco Books*, initially just to publish her own titles. Since then, however, she has produced and distributed several books by other authors.

In 2004, Jen moved back to her native Yorkshire, although she frequently returns to Cheshire, both to update and sell books, and to visit family and friends.